The Cult Fallacy: Deconstructing the Strategy and Propaganda of the Neo Salafy Cult Movement

Table of Contents

Introduction

بسم الله الرحمن الرحيم

What makes a cult? In this book you will learn everything you need to know to identify if you, or a loved one are part of the Neo Salafy cult movement. The specifics of their manipulation, bullying and mind-control tactics are outlined. Along with this their propaganda, belief system, and various inconsistencies are highlighted. The Neo Salafy Cult has become drastically weakened due to their inability to reply to their errors, or just ignore them. Since their faults are vividly described in this book you will be armed with a better understanding of what orthodox Islam is versus a Cult.

The Cult Fallacy: Deconstructing the Strategy and Propaganda of the Neo Salafy Cult Movement is a collection of 4 essays which are detailed, supported by evidences and facts to tackle the cult's movement. The case study began in 2010 and was concluded in 2018. Although the case was closed and many people left the movement, yet some still remained behind and others are joining being unaware of the real plot and the agenda of this group. Over a 30-year period this cult's movement has destroyed communities, lives, and wrecked families. Attached to this group is an alarming rate of apostasy from Islam itself for some, while other people have gone to other extremes of joining other cults outside of Islam.

Since the awareness campaign began in 2014, there has been a large amount of people who are able to completely identify them as a cult. This happened after they became aware of and read the firm literature describing the characteristics of a cult. Hence, other works might have remained undisclosed to a few. For that reason, I decided to place everything in one book for a simple reference point. At the end of this book there are some of the countless testimonies I have collected over the years of some people who left the cult, and then went on to become better human beings in society and achieve higher levels education, and stability in their life. I ask Allah to save us, our spouses and our children from being misled by doubts and desires.

Abu Aaliyah Abdullah ibn Dwight Battle

Shawwal 2nd , 1443

بسم الله الرحمن الرحيم

All Praise is for Allah alone, The Most High, and may His peace and blessing be upon the holiest Prophet and Messenger Muhammad. This treatise entitled "The Cult characteristics of, "The Salafis " in the West, A psychology case study" based on empirical data collected over a four-year period. Defined within its' content are the similarities between classic cults groups and sectarian Salafees. It expounds upon their shared traits, behavioral patterns, and tactics through the usage of Quran text, the exegesis of Muslim scholars, and the analysis of experts in the field of psychology.

Fanaticism within Islam is one of the root causes of its destruction whose fury has resulted in bloodshed amongst Muslims. It varies in extremity, with the most dangerous level being separation from the party of Allah and alignment with the party of Satan. This is the evil consequence of the ignorant that contrive principles within our blessed religion. There is a dire need to prevent this corrupt ideology from spreading and to warn of its ill affects on the ummah.

No Muslim can deny the urgency to address this issue today, as preservation of Islam, the soul, intellect, and honor and wealth of every Muslim is from the goals and objectives of the Sharia. With the consultation of scholars, students of knowledge, as well as family and friends I present this topic in

8

order to defend Islam and counsel the unenlightened.

I ask Allah to guide the readers of this work to see Salafiyah for its truth and to establish them firmly upon its implementation in every aspect of their lives. I ask Allah to forgive me for all my shortcomings and errors in my attempts to defend the blessed creed of Ahlul- Hadith.

Abu Aaliyah, Abdullah ibn Dwight Lamont Battle Jr.

M.A in Hadith and its Sciences

Doha, Qatar © Shawwal ,5th, 1435

Chapter 1 – The Existence of The Pseudo-Salafi Sect.

Shaykh Al-Islam Ibn Taymeeyah (may Allah have mercy on him) said: "Verily, many people attribute themselves to AhlusSunnah, Ahul Hadith, and Salafiyah. There are many people who attribute themselves to Imams like Ahmed and other than him, and the Aqeedah of Abu Hasan Al-Ashar'i. Nonetheless, their speech doesn't fit the criterion of the thing they affiliate themselves with. So, to have knowledge of this is a benefit." [1]

Shaykh Muhammad Raslan (may Allah preserve him) said:" Everyone who claims he adheres to Quran and Sunnah and relies on them is Salafi. However, the crucial factor lies in the facts. For that reason some scholars disliked calling themselves Salafi, or using the word, "The Salafis" or saying Salafi."[2]

Shaykh Abdus Salam ibn Burjis (d.1325H) said: "Regretfully, I must say, there are some Muslims who make Salafiyyah a Hizb like the other groups of Hizbiyah. i.e Ikhwani, Tabligh and At-Tahrir. Allah frees us from the guilt of the actions of those people. We seek refuge in Allah from the evil of their actions."

Ibn Taymiyyah said: "Any affiliation [to something] which causes disunity among the Muslims, separation from the Muslim body and causes people to divide into groups isn't allowed. This is the path of innovation and separation from the Sunnah and adherence to it. The person who affiliates himself with anything that causes partisanship is a sinner by this action, and outside of obedience to Allah and his Messenger [3]

Shaykh Muhammad ibn Salih Al- Uthaymeen said: Salafiyyah that is taken to mean a special party with specific rules whose members consider anyone who differ with them as astray, then they have nothing to do with Salafiyyah".[4]

The statements of the aforementioned scholars explicitly illustrate the presence of those who misuse the pristine title of Salafi and by it divide the Muslims into a forged hizbi sect. They, (the scholars cited) didn't dislike its affiliation in and of itself. Rather, when using the word Salafi causes people to divide into groups it becomes blameworthy, even though they carry this honorable title. Thus these people form a new group (the Salafis).[5]

Muslims are obliged to follow the Salafi methodology and turn away from everything that contradicts it. It is insufficient to assert adherence to Minhaj – As Salaf while remaining ignorant of what that entails. Thus, if a Muslim identifies himself as a Salafi he ought to have knowledge and implementation of its injunctions.

Chapter 2- The Definition of Cults and Hizbiyah

Cult: A structured group, most of whose members demonstrate unquestioned loyalty to a dynamic leader. The cult leader governs most, if not all aspects of the lives of his or her followers, often insisting that they break all ties with the world outside of them. Such groups are usually thought of in terms of religion, although other types of cults can and do exist.[6]i.e. Political, Commercial and Self Help & Counseling.[7]

The fundamental principles that define a cult are the following:

Followers of an exclusive system of religious beliefs and practices.

Obsessive, especially faddish, devotion to or veneration for a person, principle, or thing.

A religion or religious sect generally considered extremist or false.

Definition of Hizbiyah

Hizbiyah-comes from a three-letter (ح ز ب). The word Hizb means a small group.

Shaykh Muqbil ibn Hadi said: Hizbiyah is allegiance to everyone who agrees with you, and disassociation from all those who don't.[8]

Tahazzab (تحزب) means to unite for a specific cause or purpose.

Ahzab (أحزاب) are those who united against the Prophet [9].

There are two kinds of Hizbiyah:

Praiseworthy Hizbiyah: This is what represents the Muslim body as they obey the Muslim ruler. They are the party of Allah. He says:

"Verily, it is the Party of Allah that will be the successful" [Al-Mujadilah :22]

It is a must for the Muslims to adhere to this party's practices and beliefs, and defend them and advise them.

Blameworthy Hizbiyah: This occurs when one deviates from the Muslim body to another group. By following desires, they fall into division and separation from legislated guidelines. This is the party of Satan. They are identified as such since they split away from the party of Allah. Allah says:

"They are the party of Shaitan (Satan). Verily, it is the party of Shaitan (Satan) that will be the losers! [Al-Mujadila:19] [10]

From the verses referenced, it is understood that Hizbiyah is splitting and grouping that can either be commended or condemned. It is required that the Muslim holds fast to the party of Allah identified in the quoted text as "Hizb-Allah". The foundations of this party are identified in the Manhaj As- Salafi, the way in which a person truly follows footsteps of the Prophet and his companions.[11]

The pseudo Salafi is similar to a cult member; as he has an exclusive system of beliefs and practices which separate the Muslims. Additionally, he has an extreme regard for those principles.

Shaykh Muqbil said: "Our scholars in their books named others as Ahlus Sunnah and As-Salafy. Needless to say, the affair is like everything else, the actually practice of the name. You say you are Ahlul Hadith and you have no knowledge about Hadith. You claim that you are Ahlus Sunnah, while you have no desire to study the Sunnah or act by it. You declare," I am Salafi", all the while you call to the division and separation between the Muslims." [12]

Chapter 3- The origin of partisanship and its social impact.

The existence of partisanship (Hizbiyah) dates back to as early as Fir'aun. Allah says:

(Pharaoh) said: "You have believed In Him before I give You Leave. Surely, He indeed is your chief, who has taught you magic! So Verily, you shall come to know. Verily, I will cut off your hands and your feet on opposite sides, and I will crucify you all." (Ash-Shura 49)

A cult leader is considered the supreme authority of the group. This figurehead commands the upmost respect and compliance from its members and he has the only final ruling on matters. Fir'aun said:" You have believed in him before I give you leave."

He was amazed that the people believed in Allah before he allowed them or commanded them.[13]

Cults/ hizbi organizations look superb on the exterior, but internally they're very scheming and controlling. Their leaders plot franticly to deceive you and ploy you into becoming an affiliate by preying on your sincere quest for a religious connection. Once you've joined, they'll exploit you until you are no longer of any use. Their two main concerns are your wealth and time. They employ the most sophisticated psychological manipulation techniques to keep its members loyal. Don't think that you are immune from the cancerous disease of partisanship!

"Identifying with a group is the process of adopting its belief, attitudes and standards, as well as complying with its rules and regulations in effort to gain closeness to other human beings and feel part of something larger than an individual's personal life. In other words, it makes us feel like we belong."

"Each of us wants to feel like we belong somewhere. That is why groups are so important to our social lives. When we can relate to others, we are able to justify our beliefs and actions even though that justification isn't necessarily needed. "[14]

Shaykh Rabee ibn Hadi Al-Madkhali (may Allah bless him) said:

"If this grouping is built on falsehood and invites to falsehood and innovation, then it is a duty for every Muslim to say that this form of grouping isn't from Islam… Grouping for the Quran and Sunnah, making unity and separation due to the Quran and Sunnah, then this is from Islam."[15]

Chapter Four – Programming tactics and behavioral patterns

1: They claim to have truth alone.

"They say, "We believe in what was sent down to us."[Al-Baqarah :91]

2: Holding individual fanaticism and zealotry for one's party/group whether they were upon truth or falsehood was a must according to them. So Allaah revealed what He did concerning that matter

Shaykh Ahmed An-Najmi said about this point: " A person being fanatical for his group and aiding them even though they are wrong is not permissible. …It's only permissible to stand up for the truth, although that person maybe an outsider and your close relative are on falsehood. You must help the one far from you against the person dear to you by saying: "You are wrong".[16]

3: They claim to follow the Salaf (righteous predecessors), while in fact they openly oppose and contradict them.

Shaykh Zayd Al-Madkhali (Rahmatullahi) said: This applies to every innovator and misguided person who claims the call of Islam and doesn't establish it clearly with actions. In fact, his deeds and actions are in opposition to his speech (call to Dawah). This is among the issues of Jahiliyah and the methodology of the hypocrites. [17]

4: Peer pressure [18]

It's not uncommon to feel uncomfortable in a situation where our opinions and beliefs are not the same as others in our group. Do we conform, or do we hold our own? It's possible that we might just conform simply because we don't think they'll ever see our point since the odds are so stacked against us. To grasp a more vivid understanding about the dangers of peer pressure reflect on the story of Abu Talib on his death bed. He was invited to Islam, but refused after Abu Jahl and 'Abdullah ibn 'Umaya said, "O Abu Talib will you leave the religion of 'Abdul Muttalib?" Those two keep mounting that pressure on him until his final words were," I am on the religion of 'Abdul Muttalib,"

5: Hizbi groups only solicit money for their projects.

There is no cooperation or mention for any project outside of theirs. The cooperation that Islam orders is abandoned. Shaykh Muqbil said: Allah speaks about cooperation in Islam. He says: " Help you one another in Al-Birr and At-Taqwa (virtue, righteousness and piety); but do not help one another in sin and transgression.[Al-Ma'idah 2]

This means that you help every Muslim you can, regardless if he's with you or not. For example if you are the Minister of Religious Affairs and a Muslim comes to you requiring assistance, you wouldn't say, " I only help those in my group. I only help the people in my group build and furnish masjids.(This kind of person) only offers support to those in his hizb.[19]

6: Groups reject the truth from non-members based on personal issues.

" The Jews said that the Christians follow nothing (i.e. are not on the right religion); and the Christians said that the Jews follow nothing (i.e. are not on the right religion) [Al-Baqarah:113]

Both the Jews and Christian reject the truth from each other based on their feelings. This is common today among many groups that refuse to accept facts or reality from people they don't like or have personal grudges against.[20]

7: An allegiance and a disassociation from others stemming from an affiliation to the group's leaders or even followers.

Sheikh ul Islam IbnTaymiyyah said:

"No one should affiliate themselves to a sheikh, thus making friendship and enemies based on him. The Muslim must show alliance towards every person of Islam known for piety. This includes all scholars. No scholar is shown extra loyalty, unless he is known for his extra piety and faith. We give precedence to those Allah and His Messenger have. We give superiority to those Allah and His Messenger have.

Allah says:

O mankind! We have created you from a male and a female, and made you into nations and tribes, that you may know one another. Verily, the mosthonorable of you with Allah is that (believer) who has At-Taqwa [i.e. one of the Muttaqûn (pious – see V.2: 2). Verily, Allah is All Knowing, All Aware.

The Prophet said: "No Arab is superior to a Non-Arab and a Non-Arab isn't superior to an Arab. A black man is superior to a white man and vice versa, except through Taqwa."[21]

Shaykh Ali ibn Yahya Al-Hadadi (may Allah preserve him) said:

"The result of this fanaticism of the followers is love and praise (among themselves). The one who praises their leader is a beloved friend. On the contrary the one who criticizes him, even if he is correct, is a hated enemy. [22]

Among the main wicked traits of cults/Hizbi groups is that any criticism levied against them is deemed as persecution or an attack. Severe hatred towards the critic is then shown. And Allah's refuge is sought.

Imam Ash-Shawkani said:

"In reference to the enmity shown between followers of the Sunnah and innovators, then its affair is clear like the sun in the sky. Followers of the Sunnah act hostile towards the innovator due to his Bid'ah. The innovator feuds with the follower of the sunnah on account of what he follows, while the innovator believes he is correct. Thus, he clings to that innovation and becomes blind. While blinded he judges the innovated practices he follows to be entirely correct and the follower of the Quran and Sunnah is upon misguidance.[23]

Cult/ Hizbis groups focus on a living or deceased leader to whom members display excessively zealous, unquestioning commitment.

And Similarly, we sent not a warner before you (O Muhammad Sal-Allaahu 'alayheWaSallam) to any town (people) but the luxurious ones among them said: "We found our fathers following a certain Way and religion, and we will indeed follow their footsteps."

(The warner) said: "Even if I bring you better guidance than that which you found your fathers following?" they said: "Verily, we disbelieve In that with which you have been sent."[zukruf 23-24]

The Alawite Sect of Shi-ism, started by Al-Ulaya' ibn Thara'I Ad-Dawsi were from the earliest known ideologues of this wicked deviation. They hold Ali ibn Abi Talib (radi Allahu anhu) superior to Prophet Muhammad .. Their delusions even reach the peak of claiming Ali sent Muhammad to mankind, and for that reason they say Ali is God![24]

This practice was recycled to a lesser extreme among fanatical adherents of the Hanafi, Maliki, Shafa'I, and Hanbali schools of Fiqh. There are also strands of fanaticism towards the scholars that exist among certain Sufi orders. Shaykh Abu Abdul Al-'Ala Khalid ibn Uthman wrote an extensive exposition on this subject entitled "Fanaticism towards the Scholars"

All of this is rejected, as Islam is complete submission and obedience to Allah along with obedience to everything the Prophet conveyed from the Quran and authentic Sunnah.

Shaykh Muqbil (May Allah have mercy on him) said it best. "We need to be fanatical towards the Quran and Sunnah."

Cults and Hizbis are preoccupied with bringing in new members.

Shaykh Abu Abdul Al-'Ala Khalid ibn Uthman stated:

"This is among the most distinct signs of fanatics or chauvinists' people of desires and Hizbiyeen. They are proud with large numbers. Furthermore, they disparage the scholars who educate people with small numbers at their gatherings. Through large numbers Hizbis are able to swindle and mob others.

Amazingly, you'll find the cult/ Hizbi leaders angry and nauseated when invited to a gathering where small numbers are in attendance. He'll blame and scold the one responsible saying:" Why didn't you advertise this so we could have more attendees?

This character contradicts the methodology of the Salaf who feared large followings. Contemplate on the following narrations:

'Uqbah ibn Muslim said: I would give a class with one, two, three or four people, but if more came, I would remain quiet or get up and leave.

Imam Ash-Shafa'I said: It was said to Sufyan ibn Uyanah: There are people coming to see you from all over the world. Would you display anger towards them, so they return and leave you? He said they are fools- like you. They leave that which benefits them, for my bad character.[25]

There are numerous narrations that convey the displeasure the pious predecessors held for large numbers of followers. In reality, large numbers don't equate success. Cult/ hizbi groups thrive on huge followings because they generate more revenue for the movement and are a traditional tool of recruitment. Hence, they broadcast that an exuberant number showed up at their events as an enticement for others to join. The question remains how is this attendance accurately accounted for and why inform others? Is there a benefit involved for them or your society?

Shaykh Abdul Aziz Al-Bur'ee said:

"The Hizbi will always call others to his clique, regardless if it is in the invitee's well-being or not. It makes no difference if that person is a Sufi, Shia, or anything else. The Hibzi needs numbers to increase his group and then boast those numbers to others. "[26]

Sometimes the hizbi not only airs his numbers, but brags about the service he does for Allah's religion.

Ibn Aqeel said: "If you want to know the condition of Islam with the people of your era don't look at the crowds gathering at the Masjids' doors, or listen to the thunderous broadcasts about their service to Islam, but rather pay attention to their application of the Shari'ah.[27]

The Attack of Independent thought.

Cult/ Hizbi groups highly discourage independent thought and deductive reasoning. Those who question the group's motives and practices are attacked and viewed as arrogant and maybe considered as sinful. Blind, absolute acceptance of the group's positions is mandatory of its members, and any contrary belief held is considered deviance.

Shaykh Sallahudeen Muqbil Ahmed said:

"I believe whole heartedly that the scholars of Islam are the furthest from those described as those who proceeded independently in their opinions and then forced them on others. Rather they accepted the truth no matter where it came from with total honesty and complete sincerity. They acted in this manner because they knew with certainty that the truth is not restricted to anyone except the Prophet.

Abu Hanifa said: This is the opinion of An-Nu'man and whoever comes with one better, then it has more right to be adhered to."

Imam Ash-Shaf'I said: I never debated with anyone except I would say:" Oh Allah allow the truth to be in his heart and on his tongue. If the truth is with me he will follow me and if the truth is with him I will follow him."

The starting point for independent thought is justice and equity. A Muslim gives respect to the positions and religious rulings of others. Scholars differed among themselves in usul al-Fiqh (not in Aqeedah), and in subsidiary issues of fiqh; what's more is that students have differed with their teachers and Imams in various issues.

Abu Yusef and Muhammad ibn Al-Hasan Ash-Shaybani differed with their sheikh, Imam Abu Hanifah.

IbnWahhab, Ibn Al-Maajashun, and IbnAbiHazm all didn't blindly follow Imam Malik in everything he said. They differed with him in many issues and chose positions other than his.

Imam Ahmed (may Allah have mercy on him) prohibited his student from recording his opinions.

He encouraged them to rely directly on the Quran and Sunnah. [28]

4: The group is preoccupied with making money.

Cults and Hizbi groups need money to maintain its' leader's lifestyle and facilitate the expansion of its franchises and chapters. They restrict who wealth should be given to, while only mentioning their affiliates.

Allah says about money:

The life of this world is but play and pastime, but if You believe (in the Oneness of Allah Islâmic Monotheism), and fear Allâh, and avoid evil, He will grant You Your wages, and will not ask You Your wealth.

If He were to ask you of it, and press you, you would covetously withhold, and He will bring out All Your (secret) ill-wills.

Chapter Five-Programming

(The process of instructing or learning from the cult/ Hizbi)

Programming is a sequence of instructions aimed at achieving an objective. Cults/ hizbi groups utilize an array of coded propaganda to sway your sentiment and opinion in their favor until you are completely overwhelmed and in alliance with their convictions. Followers become droids of the leader's ideology, unconsciously mimicking his attitudes and attributes.The following are a list the manipulation methods contrived by cult/ hibzi factions to defeat the physique.

The group is elitist, claiming a special, exalted status for itself, its leader(s), and members.

Oh Allah protect us from the fitnah of people

A person thanks Allah and it's rejected

And a person praises someone fallaciously

Leader(s) are branded with terms like; Honorable, Noble, The Virtuous, etc. These are terms that the best of Muslims after the Prophet avoided.

Shaykh Muqbil ibn Hadi said:

 "Our societies today are ignorant about the sciences of Islam, especially the science of Jarh wa Ta'dil. People have begun to give prestigious titles to people whom guise themselves with the attire of people of knowledge. At times he might have some knowledge, but doesn't act by his knowledge. They say: The noble…. Doctor…. 'Allama, Hujjah,etc. The companions of the Prophet never addressed each other with such titles, nor are they used in their books.[29]

 This also resembles the unfounded claims of the Jews and Christians. Allah says

ÏAnd (both) the Jews and the Christians say: "We are the Children of Allâh and

his loved ones…[Al-Ma'idah 18]

Shaykh Abdur Rahman As-Sa'di said: This is the speech of both the Jews and Christians. It's a false claim wherein they pronounce for themselves integrity and credibility.[30]

Opposition Warnings

Followers are cautioned to stay away from this person, relative or friend and avoid their gatherings even though they share the same traits of piety and information. The disciple soon believes that group members and conspired, endorsed locations alone are trustworthy/truthful. The devotee doesn't take the time read or check with other reliable people of knowledge, as the names he has been given are enough.

Shaykhul Islam Ibn Taymiyah said: "Whenever a person isn't properly educated, he will always have doubt or turn away from the truth." [31]

Enemy-making and Devaluing the Outsider

Cult/ hizbi members love their affiliates simply because of fellowship and despise critics of the cult. Cult members are supposedly wonderful, moral, intelligent, and enlightened, while non-members are stupid, ignorant, immoral, and disgusting.

Those who oppose the cult's program are labeled enemies of Good. An "Us Versus Them" mindset pervades the cult and Hizbi movement. There is always a difference, usually aggrieved, between "us" and "them". Below is an unrestricted list of the vocabularies spewed against opposition:

"They" don't understand.

"They" don't know.

"They" are losers.

"They" are stupid.

"They" don't know what they are talking about.

"They" have bad motives.

"They" are all against us.

"They" are unfair to us.

"They" tell lies about us.

"They" have oppressed us.

"They" have ulterior motives.

"They" are opposed to our good works.

"They" have a hidden agenda.

"They" are trying to poison people's minds with lies about us and turn people against us.

"They" have always been trying to stop us from doing good things.

"They" are evil.

They are misguided.

They are going to the hell fire.[32]

These are some of the noted enmities building slogans listed among researchers and academics today. Moreover, you commonly hear, "They are attacking the dawah", They are trying to destroy the dawah", They are trying to take over the Dawah ", as if they are vanguards of Islam alone. Allah corrects their understanding in the following verse:

 Verily We: it is we who have sent down the Dhikr (i.e. the Qur'ân) and surely, we will Guard it (from corruption).[Al-Hijr :9]

 The programming cycle is the fertilization of elitist status for its leaders and members, succeeded by the growth of opposition- warnings and enemy making which births Totalism.

Totalism –The Us against them mentality

Everyone outside of cult/ hizbi group is lumped under one label, which strengthens group identity. This can assume deadly results for out-siders deemed enemies of their cause, leader or program. This has been identified as polarized us-versus-them mentality, which causes great conflict in society. When a cult/Hizbi member manifests this state of mind,Allah's refuge should be sought and one should steer clear of confrontation. There are noted cases of violence at the hands of those diseased with hizbiyyah .One in particular occurred in the 1990's when Shaykh Muhammad Aman Al-Jami while on the minbar, was assaulted by young followers of Sahwis in Al-Jawhara Masjid.[33]

Chapter 6- Retention (the preservation of group allegiance)

This stage illustrates how cults/Hizbi groups coerce its community to maintain attachment and dedication.

Motive Questioning:

When concrete evidence against the group is presented, members are taught to question the motivation of the presenter. The verifiable (sound documentation) is ignored because of doubts over the unverifiable (presenter's motives). Obsessive members or leaders will exclaim, "You need to know their intentions", or "They have hidden motives."

Shaykh Abu Abdul Al 'Ala Khalid ibn Muhammad ibn Uthman (may Allah reward him) said:

"This is classic sign (of a fanatic/ Hizbi). They accuse the one giving them advice as trying to turn them away from their sheikh. Subsequently, they say about the advice given, It is a lie. By this practice they follow the path of those who invented an evil method; those who disbelieved in the companions of our Messenger. Allah says:

And when Our clear Verses are recited to them, they say: "This (Muhammad Sal-Allaahu 'alayheWaSallam) is naught but a man who wishes to hinder You from that which Your fathers used to worship." and they say: "This is nothing but an invented lie." and those who disbelieve Say of the Truth when it has come to them (i.e. Prophet Muhammad Sal-Allaahu 'alayheWaSallam when Allâh sent Him as a Messenger with proofs, evidences, verses, lessons, signs, etc.): "This is nothing but evident magic!"

And we had not given them Scriptures, which they could study, nor sent to them before you (O Muhammad Sal-Allaahu 'alayhe Wa Sallam) any warner (Messenger).

Shaykh Abdur Rahman ibn Sa'di said: They said" This is his intention ", when he advised them to be sincere to Allah and leave off the customs of their fathers' whom they reverence and followed.

I (Abu Abdul Al'Ala) say: " This is what the fanatics say when you order them to be sincere to Allah and leave off the habits of their fathers and scholars whom they honor and follow without guidance".[34]

Isolation and Information Control

Shaykh Muqbil said: Hizbiyyah is isolation. Allah says in the Quran."

The believers, men and women, are Auliyâ' (helpers, supporters, friends, protectors) of one another, [At-Taubah:71]

You must help your Muslim brother if you hear he is Indonesia, even though you don't know him. The human being is the son –of- Adam and Adam was created from dirt. Help your brother whether he is an Arab or non-Arab. Allah says:

O mankind! we have created You from a male and a female, and made You into nations and tribes, that You may know one another. Verily, the Most honourable of You with Allâh is that (believer) who has At-Taqwa [i.e. one of the Muttaqûn [Al-Hujjarat 13] [35]

Shaykh Muqbil said: "The fanaticism of Hizbiyyah is isolation. The hizbi doesn't want any good for anyone other than those inside his group.[36]

Shaykh Ali Hadadi said: The innovated partisan groups today establish their group on loyalty and disloyalty based on the group. This is what dictates the interaction and relation between the individuals among the group and those outside the group.[37]

A cult/hizbi leader seeks to isolate his followers from outsiders. In the name of protecting the flock, he seeks to guarantee that his followers will only hear the group's propaganda.

The cult/hizbi leader tries to control the flow of information to his followers and between his followers. If the cult leader has his way, his followers will only hear his angle of religious teachings. All literature, books and websites are closely controlled. The cult/hizbi leader of the group will ensure as much as he can that his followers will be ingrown and inward looking by the control of authorized mailing lists and approved web sites. The cult/ hizbi leader seeks to establish a Stalinist totalitarian system that suppresses honest differences and reasonable critiques…

The cult leader entices his allies and those he considers "assets" with affection, episodic exposure in the spotlight, and the pride of being able to "rub shoulders" with the leader. These are referred to as" carrots" of position, public recognition and status.

Islam orders us to submit wholeheartedly to Allah and His Messenger and be brothers and sisters in Islam with one methodology.

" The believers are nothing else than brothers (in Islamic religion) [Al-Hujjarat 10]

"Verily, your Wali (Protector or Helper) is Allah, His Messenger, and the believers." [Al-Ma'idah 55]

If the isolation process doesn't work there is information control. Information control among cult/hizbi circles is built on various key elements: Among the most commonly used today are:

 Deception- Cult members will often:

Deliberately withhold information from recruits.

Distort information to make it appear acceptable.

Lie to obtain their goal.

Shaykh Abu Abdul Al-'Ala Khalid Uthman said: Their irrational devotion causes them to piece up information then embellish it with lies in order to make their Shaykh's image pleasant in front of others.[38]

 Forbiddance of Outside source Information- Acquiring information outside of the group source is minimized or discouraged. These restrictions are set on:

Certain books, articles, newspapers, magazines, TV and radio shows that expose the group.

Critical information pertaining to the internal problems within the group.

Written critiques, letters, editorials, or history of involvements of former members of the group.

Websites.

Spying and Surveillance

Following affiliates and opposition accounts through Facebook, Twitter and Emailing list to monitor and control.

Reporting deviant thoughts, feelings, and actions to leadership by way of screenshots, copy and paste images, etc.

Group Propaganda

Newsletters, magazines, journals, audiotapes, videos, tweets, etc. are utilized for the hyperactivity centered around the group

Misquotations, statements taken out of context from non-cult sources and non-cult members.

Creation of multiple websites to cartel information.

Unconfidently Confession

Information about "sins" is used to abolish identity boundaries.

Past "sins" are exposed to manipulate and control; no forgiveness or absolution is given. This is done to members and critics of the group. A public repentance is demanded, which isn't done for the pleasure of Allah, but to remain closeness to the group and prove loyalty. [39]

Through info regulation the group establishes its mighty presence and constructs a towering wall of intimidation. The desired benefit is revenue, expansion, and monopoly. This scandalous act is perpetrated in the disguise of feigned sincerity andin the name of pure Islam.

Shaykh Muqbil ibn Hadi said:

"Stop deceiving people in the name of Islam. Don't deceive people with using the name Sunnah. The Sunnah nowadays has become like a Jubba.[40] A person wears if he wants to and takes it off when he wants to. Stop deceiving people in the name of Salafiyah!

We don't claim we alone own the title Sunnah and Salafiyah. In reality, Salafiyah is to return to methodology the salaf practiced Islam. Was Imam Al-Bukhari a Hizbi? Did Imam Ahmed have group? Was Abdullah ibn Al-Mubarak with a faction? Did Sa'eedibn Al-Musayib have a clique? Was Abu Hurayrah part of a group? Was Abu Bakr a Hizbi? They were not Hizbis. They invited others to the Quran and Sunnah. When the time came for Jihad they went out and fought. Abdullah ibn Al-Mubark spent an entire year as solider on post, and the following year he made Hajj and gave lessons. This is the affair of our salaf.

Don't swindle people by using the name As-Salafiyah or As-Sunnah. You are far from the reality of the Sunnah and As-Salafiyah. You have become Hizbiyeen. You scam people by using Ayah from the Quran and Hadith from the Prophet.[41]

Shaykh Muqbil plainly stated that he didn't own the Sunnah or Salafiyyah. This message of Islam is a free invitation to anyone who wants to hear it. It makes no difference in which state, country or continent they reside in. Shaykh Muqbil words are comprehensible. You have people who swindle people in the name of As-Salafiyah. So be wise!

Coercion to facilitate FEAR

When confronted by peer pressure, we often resort to unsound judgment. Our behavior is affected not by our sound beliefs and attitudes, but by social coercion. We act under the presumption of what others might think of us. Disagreement with the group's position or the leader's ideas can result in expulsion and shunning. Bear in mind that a hizbi has been a follower of this group for some time, hence, he is fearful! He asks himself where will I go? Who will talk to me, what about my friends? Furthermore, if he has an established business within the recluse community, then he faces the possibility of losing support.

Cults /Hizbi leaders are attributed with piety and subsequently; complete loyalty is due to him. Failure to do so is distorted into misguidance or sin. A Perfect example of this is found in the story of Musa and Fir'uan.

Allah says:

(65. They said:"O Mûsa (Moses)! either You throw first or we be the first to throw?"

[Mûsa (Moses)] said: "Nay, throw You (first)!" Then behold, their ropes and their sticks, by their magic, appeared to Him as though they moved fast.

So Mûsa (Moses) conceived a fear In himself.

we (Allâh) said: "Fear not! surely, You will have the upper hand.

"And throw that which is In Your Right hand! it will swallow up that which they have made. that which they have made is Only a magician's trick, and the magician will never be successful, no matter whatever amount (of skill) He may attain."

So, the magicians fell down prostrate. they said: "We believe In the Lord of Hârûn (Aaron) and Mûsa (Moses)."

[Fir'aun (Pharaoh)] said: "Believe You in Him [Mûsa (Moses)] before I give You Permission? Verily! He is Your chief who taught You magic. So, I will surely cut off Your hands and feet on opposite sides, and I will surely crucify You on the trunks of date-palms, and You shall surely know which of us [I (Fir'aun Pharaoh) or the Lord of Mûsa (Moses) (Allâh)] can give the Severe and more lasting torment."

they said: "We prefer You not over the clear signs that have come to us, and to Him (Allâh) who created us. So decree whatever You desire to Decree, for You can Only decree (regarding) This life of the world.

"Verily! we have believed In Our Lord, that He may forgive us Our faults, and the magic to which You did compel us. And Allâh is better as regards reward In comparison to Your [Fir'aun's (Pharaoh)]

Reward, and more lasting (as regards punishment In comparison to Your punishment)."

Verily! whoever comes to his Lord as a Mujrim (criminal, polytheist, disbeliever In the Oneness of Allâh and his Messengers, sinner, etc.), Then surely, for Him is Hell, therein He will neither die nor live.

but whoever comes to Him (Allâh) as a believer (in the Oneness of Allâh, etc.), and has done righteous good deeds, for such are the High ranks (in the Hereafter),

'Adn (Edn) Paradise (everlasting Gardens), under which rivers flow, wherein they will abide forever: such is the reward of those who purify themselves [(by abstaining from All kinds of sins and evil deeds) which Allâh has forbidden and by doing All that which Allâh has ordained)].

These preceding verses show that when a leader has followers to whom the truth concerning him has been made clear, he becomes hostile. They are able to see the reality of his falsehood and his last resort is fear, as his argument has been demolished.

Allah says:

The magicians fell down and prostrated to Allah prompting Fir'aun to remind them that he was their leader. When he saw them firm with conviction, he threatened to cut off their hands and feet. Having trust and faith in Allah they responded to his intimidation tactic by saying:" We prefer You not over the clear signs that have come to us, and to Him (Allâh) who created us. So, decree whatever You desire to Decree, for You can Only decree (regarding) This life of the world."

Look how they followed the truth when it came to them in the face of adversity! Which cult/ Hzibi leader today has the power Fir'aun possessed? Cult/ hizbi members possess deficiency in their Iman. Allah's help is sought.

Chapter 7- Mind Control techniques

Brainwashing is a theoretical indoctrination process that results in an impairment of autonomy, an inability to think independently, and a disruption of beliefs and affiliations. In other words, you are being told what to think, who to talk to and what to believe from the Cult/ Hizb leader or followers. Once spell stricken, the partisan group leader can convince you to believe the unfathomable.

Ad hominem (Latin) means "against the man". As the name suggests, it is a literary term that involves commenting on or against an opponent to undermine him instead of his arguments. There are cases where consciously or unconsciously people start to question the opponent or his personal association rather than evaluating the soundness and validity of the argument that he presents. Cult/hizbis groups use the fallacy of character assassination as a tool to deceive their audience. Making such a blatant personal comment against somebody makes it hard for people to believe it isn't true. One of the main benefits Cult/Hizbi groups gain from this principle is distancing its followers away from valid criticisms against themselves.

An example of this relates to Nuh's people. Allah says:

"The people of Nuh (Noah) denied (their Messenger) before them, they rejected Our slave, and said: "A madman!" and he was insolently rebuked and threatened [Al-Qamar 9]

Shaykh Islam Ibn Taymiyah said: They described him as being ignorant. They said he was a madman. When people describe a person as being a madman, it's known if he is sensible or insane about his speech and actions. [42]

When they are unable to address the issue, they attack the character.

Finger Pointing:
Finger pointing is creating a false sense of righteousness by pointing to the shortcomings of the outside world and other non-affiliates of the cult/ Hizbi group. This induces naïve members of the group to avoid people without just cause, while at the same time gaining an unrefined faction.

Ibn Jawzi said: "The most diseased form of backbiting is when people induce others to stay away from other people and look towards them. They combine the acts of dispraising the one in mention and earning praise for themselves. Due to their ignorance, they are oblivious to fact that they are falling into two sins: backbiting and showing off (Riya). For example, a person is mentioned within their circle and they say: "Praise to Allah we have no concern to visit the Sultan and strive for the vanities of this world.", or they say about him, "We seek refuge in Allah from deficient modesty, we ask Allah to save us from being immodest." With these words their intention is to instruct someone to see the shortcomings of someone else. [43]

Conspired endorsements:

The group/leader is the exclusive means of knowing "truth" or receiving validation, no other process of discovery is really acceptable or credible. They only accept the praise or the criticism from their Shaykh, or from the people their Shaykh has praised.

Shaykh Abu Abdul 'Al-Ala said:

"The only person criticized in their view is the one their scholar has criticized. If the criticism is general and rejected, due to a detailed praise from a number of scholars, you'll find they won't pay any attention to what those ulema have said. i.e the detailed praised. They say: "Our shaykh is more knowledgeable about the condition of such and such than those scholars. The detailed criticism takes precedence over the general praise." This is what those people negligent or ignorant say! This is a correct principle. The detailed criticism takes precedence over the general praise. Furthermore, if you investigate the situation, you'd find that this criticism is based on false reports and hidden hatred or envy. This criticism isn't supported by knowledge -based research. Ibn Abdul Bar (May Allah have mercy on him) said: "A group of

45

scholars in Fiqh and Hadeeth, who have insight in understanding and research have said: "We don't accept (the Jarh) from Ibn Ma'een or other people about a person who is well known for knowledge, trustworthiness, and sound understanding. The criticism in this case is rejected until the reason he's criticizing the Muslim is in accordance with the actions that validate a trustworthy person to be criticized. Reason being, this person is marked as being reliable. Therefore, it's incorrect to think about him being otherwise." [TamheedDarulFarquq 7/171]

Shaykh Khalid ibn Muhammad Uthman said: "If this type of criticism isn't accepted from someone like Ibn Ma'een, except with a valid reason, then what about someone less than him in our era?!" The praise of that person from the senior scholars is based on their experience with him, their relationship with him, and their knowledge about his Minhaj[methodology]. Moreover, their detailed praise concerning him is based on their awareness of his actions, which prove his honesty from lies and attest to his sound Minhaj. Nonetheless, despite all this you find those fanatics rejecting the praise from the major scholars for that individual. They hold only the words of their shaykh as being sufficient. They spread their scholar's criticism (against the person) everywhere heedlessly and ignorantly. Consequently, they make their scholar the leader of their party. He has the right to say who gets membership and who doesn't. He has the right to say who is on it and who's off it without proof. And no doubt this is ghuloo.[44]

Chapter 8- Conclusion.

Cults and Hizbiyyah are very real observable facts in the World today. Thousands of people have become involved with these movements. The tragedy is that everybody is negatively affected by their membership. The Cults/Hizbi groups that exist today are basically pyramid shaped dictatorial regimes with a person or group that has demanding control.

The processes defined all through this paper are the causes of disorder in the individual's life. This disorder has a dramatic impact on the Muslim's personality and practice of Islam. Eventually, if there is no intervention in the person's life he could become a complete separatist in society and have negative views about life in general thus aggressive and Allah's help is sought.

Isn't it time we wake up and smell the coffee and ignore the Cult/Hizbi recruitment and movements? Isn't the path clear for us to follow? Why must we continue to rely on those who have no concern for quality education? How much more time are we going to waste following the miscellaneous information that's disseminated? More importantly, how much longer before our deeds stop and the questioning begins?

Islam is a self-governing system granted to the human being by Allah's Mercy with communal responsibility. Allah informed us that we are the best nation brought forth from mankind. We enjoin what is right and forbid what is wrong. The self-governing ordinance doesn't allow separatism nor does the communal aspect promote gang culture. Hizbiyah is devotion of both aspects, amazement with one's self fostered by a false sense of piety and gross misunderstanding of the Islamic concept of unity.

Division is Shaytaan's weapon and self-amazement is his despicable disposition, so the very nature of hizbiyyah is his methodology. His throne is above water desiring the separation of man from his wife. You, you're the one!

Prepared by

Abu Aaliyah Abdullah ibn Dwight Battle

Chapter 9- References

[1] SharulAsfahaniyah 205-206

[2] Daa'aim minhajun Nabuwa, page 166, by shaykh Rslan.

[3]majmu' al Muhadarat fee mayaksu dawah 81, vol 3]

[4]Allama ibn Uthaymeen ,Liqaa-al-Baab Al-Maftooh Q# 1322

[5]Shaykh Rslan , page 166

[6]Read more: Cults – Psychology Encycledia, Charismatic, and People – JRank Articleshttp://psychology.jrank.org/pages/160/Cults.html#ixzz38sYg9z62

[7]http://psychology.jrank.org/pages/160/Cults.html

[8]http://www.muqbel.net/fatwa.php?fatwa_id=156

[9]Mukhtar As-sahhaah , Imam Muhammad ibnAbiBakrAr-Razi 84,

[10] Al-Amru bi
Lazumi jamahatil muslimeen wa imamuhum ,by Abdus Salam ibn Burjis(1425H) page 64

[11] Da'aim minhajun nubuwa page 165 by , Shaykh Rslan,

[12] Gharatu Al-Ashrata vol 1/page 200

[13] Taysirul Kareem Ar-Rahman , By Shaykh Abdur Rahman As-Sa'di vol3/424, 1st edition, (Beirut : Darul Fikr 1410)

[14] The everything Psychology book, Lynda L. Warwci Ph.D., Lesly Bolton, page 233

[15] page112Jama'atuWahidatun la Jama'at wa SIratun Wahidun la Ash-sharat , By Shaykh Rabee ibn Hadi Al-Madkhali, Printed my Maktabatul Ghurabah wal Athariyah, 2nd edition 1418H)

[16] Al-Amaali An-Najmeeyah ala Mas'il Al-Jahileeyah, by Shaykh Ahmed An-Najmi, page 114-115m DarulManhaj 1434H

[17] Al-Fawa'id Al-Jaliyah Sharhu Masa'ili Al-Jahiliyah, by Shaykh Zayd Madkhali, page 279,

[18] (page 226-227 The Everything Psychology book)

[19] Gharatu Al-Ashratah vol2/page 25, by Shaykh Muqbil

[20] Sharun Masa'il Jahiliyah, By Shaykh Salih Al Ash-Shaykh page 161-165, printed by Darus Salafyah 1st edition 1431H

[21] Shaykhul Islam ibn Taymiyyah, Fatawa Al-Iraqiyah, vol 1/page 91-91, Printed by Maktabutul Islamiyyah(1st edition Beirut 1425H)

[22] Al-Ghulu wa Mathahirahu feel Hayati Al-Muasra,,by, Ali ibn Yahya Al-Hadadi. page 69, Printed Darul Minhaj 1st edition 2005

[23]Qatrul Waliala Hadith al-Wali page 275 .

[24] Page. 284 Mu'jam Al-fath Al-Aqeedah.

[25]At-
Ta'asub lil shaykukh awatifu Mashubag bil Ahwa, by shaykh Abu Abdul' 'Ala Khalid ibnUthman, page 162

[26]At-Ta'leeq ala Shartil Hizbiyyah, page 72, by Abdul Azeez ibn Yahya Al-Bur'I ,Darul Haramain 1421H

[27] Abadus Shari'ah 1/268

[28]page 299-301/Zawabi' fee Wajhi Sunnati Qadeeman wa Hadeethan , printed by Daru Alimil Kutub , reviewed by Shaykh Rabee ibn Hadi Al-Madkhali (may Allah bless him)

[29]Shaykh Muqbil ibn Hadi , page 21, Al-MukhrajuMinal Fitnah.5th edition, Darul Haramain 1420H

[30]Tafsir As-Sad'Ivol 1/ page 460, by Shaykh Abdur Rahman As-Sa'di, Printed by Darul Fikr, Beirut Lebanon 1st edition 1415H

[31] An-Nabuwat vol2/ 607, by Shaykhul Islam ibn Tayimiyah, printed by Darul Ibn Abbass 2006

[32]http://www.orange-papers.org/orange-cult_q8.html

[33]Here   is   the   youtube
: http://www.youtube.com/watch?v=vmOCB3w4V
Co video to hear the attack against the shaykh.
Recently, Dr Khalid Ar-Raddadi mentioned that a
person was dragged out of the Prophet's masjid and
beaten. The accounts of such incidences recorded
are enormous, but I refrained from mentioning them
as some have publicly made Tawbah.

[34]At-Ta'asub lil shaykuk awatifu Mashubug bil
Ahwa, by shaykh Abu Abdul' 'Ala Khalid ibn
Uthman, page 147

[35] Ghratu Al-Ashrata vol2/pg 93

[36] Gharatu Al-Ashrata vol2/26

[37] Ali hadadi /page 70

[38] At-Ta'asubu lil Shayukh, by Shaykh Khalid
Uthman, page 280

[39]http://www.orange-papers.org/orange-
cultinfo.html#information

[40]Jubba(a long outer garment open in the front
with wide sleeves[Hans Wehr]

[41]126-127,   QamulMu'anidwazajrulHaqidi   al-
Hasidi,   By   shaykhMuqbilIbnHadi   Al-Wadi,
printed,1422, MaktabatusSan'a , Ta'iz , Yemen.
1422H

[42] An-Nubuwat 1/143, Ibn Taymiyyah.

[43]MinhajulQasideen , by IbnJawzi vol2/pg 680

[44]At-
Ta'asub lil shaykukh awatifu Mashubag bil Ahwa,
by shaykh Abu Abdul' 'Ala Khalid ibn Uthman,
page144

[45] . Shaykh-ul-Islām Ibn Taymiyyah: Many
people test these groups based on suspicion and
desires; thus, they place their group and those who
affiliate with their followers and support them as
being among Ahl-us-Sunnah. On the other hand
everyone who opposes them is considered Ahl-ul-
Bid'ah [Majmū' al-Fatāwā [3/346-347]

Essay 2 - Propaganda Pundits Masquerading the Salafi Dawah

بسم الله الرحمن الرحيم

My dearest Muslim,

As you are well aware, the illustrious compiler of
hadith Abu Hurayrah (may Allah be pleased with
him) conveyed that our beloved Prophet
Muhammad (may the peace and blessings of Allah
be upon him) said, "The believer does not allow
himself to be stung twice from the same
hole."[1] Ibn Hajar, (may Allah have mercy upon
him) commenting on this narration in Fathul-Barri
stated, "Stinging is done by poisonous insects or

creatures that crawl."[2] Al-Khattabi (may Allah have mercy on him) mentioned in 'Alamu As-Sunan, "As for the Prophet's saying: "should not be stung", this is a command in the form of a statement which means that a believer should be watchful and should not be taken suddenly time after time. This may be done in matters of the religion as it is in worldly affairs; and the affairs of the religion are more important."[3] Thus, as Muslims we are to be resolutely aware of being victimized by deception. Our intelligence must prevail over apathy in order for reoccurring injury to be avoided.

In light of the prophetic exhortation to safeguard oneself from harm prescribed in the aforementioned hadith, and my sincerest wish for our collective well-being, I advise myself, you, and our brothers of Salafi Publications along with their affiliates concerning the venomous, propaganda, tabloid tactics they utilize in attempt to monopolize and control Salafiyyah in the West.

Propaganda is neutrally defined as a systematic form of purposeful persuasion that attempts to influence the emotions, attitudes, opinions, and actions of specified target audiences for ideological, political, or commercial purposes through the controlled transmission of one-sided messages (which may or may not be factual) via mass and direct media channels.[4] It has been utilized throughout history by agencies to manipulate and sway the general public in support of their varying agendas. Prominent examples familiar to those residing in western societies are the smear campaigns used by political candidates to discredit their opponents during elections, or the celebrity endorsement of products to entice consumers toward its purchase.

Be aware my honorable brothers and sisters in faith, that Satan (may Allah curse him) was the first propagandist. He belligerently schemed against Adam and Hawaa (may Allah's peace be upon them) coercing them into disobedience through his distortion that consuming from the tree Allah forbade them would render them angelic or grant them immortality. Allah says, "Then Satan began to whisper suggestions to them, in order to reveal to them their shame that was hidden from them before. He said, "Your Lord only forbade you this tree, lest you become angels or beings that live forever." And he (Satan) swore by Allah to them both (saying), "Verily, I am one of the sincere well-wishers for you both. So, he misled them with deception. Then when they tasted of the tree, that which was hidden from them of their shame (private parts) became manifest to them and they began to stick together the leaves of Paradise over themselves (to cover their shame). And their Lord called out to them (saying), "Did I not forbid you that tree and tell you: Verily, Satan is an open enemy unto you? "They said, "Our Lord! We have wronged ourselves. If You forgive us not, and bestow not upon us Your Mercy, we shall certainly be of the losers." (Allah) said: "Get down, one of you an enemy to the other [i.e. Adam, Hawwa (Eve), and Shaitan (Satan), etc.]. On earth will be a dwelling-place for you and an enjoyment, for a time."[5]

It is through the stratagem of purposeful persuasion that Satan gains temporary mastery over the heart and intellect of the Sons of Adam. We must be cognizant that the Quran is the utmost authority regarding human nature and its altering physical and psychological conditions. Allah vividly illustrated the discourse between Our Father and his sworn enemy to evidence our weakness. Allah states," Should not the One who created know? And He is The Subtle, The Aware"[6] and He also says, "We have explained in detail in this Quran for the benefit of mankind every kind of similitude, but man in most things is contentious."[7]

Modern psychology in its finite inquiry, has sought to define the models and tactics employed by propagandists, only to be preceded and outranked by the divine revelation of the Quran. Utilizing the Book of Allah and its scholarly exegesis as the primary source of disputation, and contemporary psyche research as evidence to establish the superiority of Allah's word as well a sociological reference, I've detailed the blatant tabloid schemes of Spubs and the nuances of their propaganda exploits.

The most primitive and over-abused tactic of propagandists is the usage of derogatory names to belittle or humiliate an opponent. Allah says, "And they say: You (Muhammad) to whom the Dhikr (the Qur'an) has been sent down! Verily, You are a mad man." [8] Allah also informs, "Likewise, no Messenger came to those before them, but they said: "A sorcerer or a madman!"[9] Propagandists engage opposition in this vituperative manner to discredit the validity of the argument waged against them. Slandering causes fear and mistrust; thus is a profitable way to alter perception and avoid constructive debate. It is desired that their audience will reject the disputant on the basis of description with negative connotation instead of investigating the evidence presented.

Spubs, its cohorts, and followers habitually employ this lowly and despicable practice abhorred by Allah as He stated, "O you who have believed, let not a people ridicule [another] people; perhaps they may be better than them; nor let women ridicule [other] women; perhaps they may be better than them. And do not insult one another and do not call each other by [offensive] nicknames. Wretched is the name of disobedience after [one's] faith. And whoever does not repent – then it is those who are the wrongdoers.[10] The Messenger of Allah (May the peace and blessings of Allah be upon him) said congruently: "Insulting a Muslim is immoral conduct (fisq) and fighting him is disbelief (kufr)."[11] Some of the common slurs hurled by this diseased group are: liar, donkey, affiliate of X, Y, or Z, fame-seeker, deviant, dajjal, Iblis, supporter of deviants, ahmaq (Fool), unknown, impostor, pretender, coward, resentful hater, arrogant, idiot, fraud, moron and feign knowledge.[12] Sufficient is Allah as a witness to their manifest deviation from his legislation.

We must be conscious as seekers of truth that Allah cautions, "O you who believe! Be not like those who annoyed Musa (Moses), but Allah cleared him of that which they alleged, and he was honorable before Allah."[13] The Messenger of Allah (May the peace and blessings of Allah be upon him) expounded on this verse stating: "The (people of) Bani Israel used to bathe naked (all together) looking at each other. The Prophet Moses used to bathe alone. They said, 'By Allah! Nothing prevents Moses from taking a bath with us except that he has a scrotal hernia.' So once Moses went out to take a bath and put his clothes over a stone that ran away with them. Moses followed that stone, saying, 'my clothes, O stone! My clothes, O stone!' till the people of Bani Israel saw him and said, 'By Allah, Moses has no defect in his body." [14]

The circulation of false accusations, fostering rumors, and manipulating information are weapons used by propagandist assassins to destroy the reputation and credibility of an individual or institution. Methodically, Spubs company spies pillage through the lives, social media accounts, and works of those they collectively target on a frantic paparazzi-like scavenger hunt for any viable scrap of info and misconstrue it into a blazing arrow of defamation aimed at breaking the honor of the innocent. The Messenger of Allah (May the peace and blessings of Allah be upon him) said, "Beware of suspicion, for suspicion is the worst of false tales; and do not look for others' faults and do not spy, and do not be jealous of one another, and do not desert (cut your relation with) one another, and do not hate one another; and O Allah's worshipers! Be brothers (as Allah has ordered you)."[15] Ibn Taymiyyah said, "Name calling and character assassination isn't knowledge nor is it beneficial"[16] and Ibn Qayyim Al-Jawziyyah declared, "Whoever treads the path of the Messenger and his companions, let him get used character assassination and slander from Ahl Bid'ah. The people of innovation will conduct fault findings in order to turn people away from him." [17]

Rumors and gossip are public nuisances that menace one's honor, family, and livelihood. Its influence poisons relationships and is noxious to the well-being of communal life. Both cling to invention and deceit, and even though containing grains of truth, are malignant. Allah states: "When you were propagating it with your tongues, and uttering with your mouths that whereof you had no knowledge, you counted it a little thing, while with Allah it was very great![18] Abdul-Ghani Al-Maqdasi said: Undoubtedly, being preoccupied with circulating bad news, magnifying people's mistakes, and determined to hunt and follow up on one's errors spreads disorder and causes stress. As a result of this culture, people become frustrated and hopeless. This increases fitnah people easily to fall victim to.[19] Circulating rumors is one of the main branches of propaganda resorted to when one desires relevancy or is critiqued but unqualified to respond tactfully. He strives feverishly to divert the public from the main and crucial issues though his objective isn't to make you believe the speculation, but to implant false memories about their relevant enemies and maintain anti- social behavior.

Spubs' mastery of diversion is greatly exemplified in their rebuttal to The Cult Characteristics of the Salafees in The West. Raha Batts, a self-confessed penitentiary educated convert whose integrity and proficiency at translating has been previously challenged,[20] penned an English translation of a phone call placed to Sheikh Khalid Uthman of Egypt whose book "Fanaticism towards the Scholars" was cited in my research. An endorsement was sought from Sheikh Khalid to discredit the validity of my findings through his testimonial, a propaganda technique frequently used in advertising where a noted personality is sought to support or promote a person, group, or product.

The headline reads:

"SHEIKH KHALID UTHMAAN: IBN DWIGHT BATTLE HAS NO RIGHT TO MISUSE THE SPEECH OF THE SCHOLARS TO ACCUSE SALAFEES IN THE WEST OF HIZBIYYAH BECAUSE THEY MAKE ITTIBAA' OF THE SCHOLARS."[21]

Our brother Raha, (may Allah grant him honesty and knowledge) resorts to sensationalism, the usage of exciting or shocking stories or language at the expense of accuracy, in order to provoke public interest or excitement. The colon placed after the sheikh's name is used to separate an independent clause from a quotation, thus indicating that the phrase that followed is his (sheikh Khalid's) actual speech. Yet after thorough examination, you'll find this quote is absent from the text of the conversation. This is because Raha blatantly exaggerated the sheikh's words and hoped that his craftiness would avoid the keen eye. Sheikh Khalid per the article clearly stated: "This man has no right to apply MY SPEECH which is for fanatics, to the Salafees", and not the speech of "THE SCHOLARS."

This subtle bandwagon strategy is an attempt to persuade the target audience to join in and pursue the course of action that seemingly the majority (the scholars) has chosen. The intentional vagueness of the term "the scholars" implies that topic being addressed is collectively shared information and creditable to be accepted as a consensus (ijmaa). Such a title is enough to arouse the naïve layman sincerely seeking truth to follow suit, however it is completely unrecognizable whom exactly "The Scholars" includes. Yazid ibn Habib said, "The scholars say the mother is superior to the father in regards to all rights."[22] Take notice to how he used "the scholars" for an issue agreed upon by consensus.

Furthermore, Sheikh Khalid said, "I say, firstly, I do not know this man. This man is unknown to me; I do not know him" which is factual, yet the conniving headline schemed by Raha suggests that he and I are on a first name basis. The Cult characteristics of the Salafees in the West is a synthesis of the expression of many scholars, therefore the exclusion of the statements of one wouldn't jeopardize its integrity, nor challenge its validity. Raha understood this and found no other way to discredit it except through deception. Ibn Qayyim said, "Whoever contemplates over each and every misleading article of falsehood and innovation will discover that its author phrases it nicely and garbs it with words that will make it acceptable to people who don't know the reality of the issue addressed."[23]

Moreover, it is evident that Sheikh Khalid's assertion was conditional. He states, "If they are those who are true Salafees," which disassociates him from liability of the motivation behind the questioning which is skeptical, due to Raha concealing that I didn't mention any specific group. Rigorous honesty must be employed as opposed to selective amnesia when soliciting verdicts from the scholars. Cherry picking is the act of highlighting individual cases or data that seem to confirm a particular position, while ignoring or suppressing a significant portion of related cases or data that may be in contradiction. Allah says, "And mix not truth with falsehood, nor conceal the truth"[24] and "Know they not that Allah knows what they conceal and what they reveal?"[25] Shaykhul Islam Ibn Taymiyyah stated, "Among the signs of Ahl Bid'ah is they narrate what's for them and conceal what is against them."[26]

There are in fact many entities that claim Salafiyyah in the West, yet Spubs alone crudely expressed contention with my research. Allah says: "They think every cry is against them!"[27] I specifically addressed a "Salafee cult." If the descriptions provided are qualities that they don't possess, then there would be absolutely no need to respond. Simple retrospection will lead you to conclude that they've made innovators of everyone except themselves, so inherently they are "THE SALAFEES", a sentiment justly rebutted by Allah's statement: "And don't sanctify yourselves, He (Allah) knows best who has taqwaa."[28] Crowning themselves and their affiliates as the only Salafees has essentially made allegiance to them a condition of Salafiyyah.[29]

The Invocation of righteousness is a delusion of grandeur suffered by nations past. Allah revealed, "And (both) the Jews and the Christians say: "We are the children of Allah and His loved ones."[30] Mujirudeen ibn Muhammad Al- Maqdasi (may Allah have mercy upon him) explained, "The meaning here is that Allah is like a father in compassion and mercy. They are his children and have the status of a child to his father in closeness."[31] Al-Allamah Abdullah Ad- Duwaysh (may Allah have mercy upon him) said, "invoking the righteous call is frequently found with people who deviate from the straight path of those who have knowledge, are poor, and firm in their worship. As result of this deviation, they fall into innovation and misguidance. Through using the elitist status, they desire to be known and respected, so they love to be praised for that which they don't do from their followers. Elitist status gives them a reputation of being sincere and knowledgeable."[32] The fallacies of their self-indulgence forge the assumption that any challenge to them is immoral and any criticism is an unwarranted attack. Allah says: "Have you not seen those who claim sanctity for themselves. Nay, but Allah sanctifies whom He pleases"[33] Al-Qurtubi (may Allah have mercy upon him) said, "the meaning of this verse is, don't attest piety to yourselves that your righteous and free of sin and disobedience. Allah is fully aware of the person fearing his punishment, so avoid sinning."[34] Allah also states, "And never think that those who rejoice in what they have perpetrated and like to be praised for what they did not do – never think them [to be] in safety from the punishment, and for them is a painful punishment."[35]

The genesis of their illusion and aberration is the deficiency and disparagement of education. There has emerged from this small, homogenous group a disturbing irreverence toward Islamic university credential. Ironically, there are countless Salafi scholars, professors, and students who possess degrees. Amongst those prominent are, Dr. Abdus Salam Burjis, Dr. Salih Al-Fawzan, Dr. Rabee Al-Madkhali, Dr. Saalih As-Suhaymi, Dr. Falah Ismail Al-Mandakar, Dr. Muhammad Raslan, Dr. Muhammad Bazmoul, Dr. 'Alee Naasir Al-Faqeehee, and Dr. 'Abdur-Razzaaq Al-'Abbaad. It is imperative to highlight that the acquisition of a degree doesn't conclude that its possessor has knowledge, though according to Dr. Fowzan he is a certified to teach while the one without license needs tazkiyah.

Spubs has sewn together a patchwork conglomerate of narcissistic, scarcely educated men of hive like mentality who lean heavily on antiquated commendations that have been tarnished by repetitious accusations of infidelity and insubordination. Those thoroughly educated and progressive are a direct threat to their relevancy, which is why they are so viscerally demeaned. It is incumbent upon us as owners of intellect to interrogate ourselves as to the validity of an Islamic education that comprises of extremely short-term study in Yemen, Egypt, or Saudi Arabia that occurred in some cases 10, 15, or even 20 years ago, and how the status as a student of knowledge is preserved if one hasn't returned to its path since then. Allah states, "I take Allah's Refuge from being among Al-Jahilun (the ignorant or the foolish)." [36]Al-Khalil ibn Ahmed (may Allah have mercy upon him) said, "There are three out four kinds of people you can speak to. A man who knows and recognizes he has knowledge, so speak to him. A man who has knowledge, but he believes that he doesn't, accordingly speak to him. A man doesn't know and is aware of the fact that he has no knowledge, so speak to him. Then there is a person who has no knowledge, but he believes he is knowledgeable, don't speak to him." [37]

To disguise their inadequacies and masquerade as students of knowledge, Spubs have exploited the scholars to perpetuate a culture of fear, a term defining the incitement of terror in the general public to achieve political or religious superiority. Fear is the fastest way to bypass rationale, and when logical deduction is lost, one will believe anything. Allah says, "Yet they try to frighten you with those besides Him! And whom Allah sends astray, for him there will be no guide." [38] Sheikh Muhammad Lowh (May Allah preserve him) said, "The sheikh who they reverence contains the climate of fear. They encircle their group and population with fear so much so that their community refuses to have anything to do with critics (outside the circle). The critics explain the truth and steer people to worship Allah alone without any partners. You will notice that they use any means of fear feasible to divert them away from the critics' advice and guidance." [39]

At a seminar hosted by Al-Furqan in June of 2014 wittingly entitled "The sickness and the cure" Abu Muhammad Al-Magribi exclaimed, "I'm not playing no games! I didn't play games before; I was patient with certain people. If I catch anyone interfering with the dawah and he's not fit, I have two words for him. I'm going to report you to the ulema, bottom line with your name, with your real name! I'm going to find your real name and I'm gonna call Shaykh Rabee. Shaykh Rabee, this is a person who's interfering with Dawah."[40]

Under whose jurisdiction was he deputized as an intelligence agent of moral authority, sanctioned to critique and flaunt his findings? Allah orders, "And speak good to people." Intimidation is incompatible with the Prophet's call, (may the peace and blessings of Allah be upon him) and is an aversion to an audience seeking morality.

A Frankenstein has been erected from the knowledge, honor, and astuteness of the scant number of scholars they resort to with Dr. Rabee being the head of their monster. The mere mention of his name was once the source of despair for those they threatened and bullied, but due to their intemperate abuse of his merit its effectiveness has waned and likened him in public view to a repudiated crime boss.

Their unwavering loyalty and devotion to him spawned a cult of personality, subsequently basing allegiance and disassociation on his dynamism. This mentality is an infamous trait of the Sufi cult. Abdul-Qadir Al-Jaylani believed that the disciple must never disagree with his sheikh outwardly, and had to stay clear of opposing him even in his heart and mind. The obligation to follow those who exhort towards truth is undeniable however, we don't believe anyone after the Prophet (may the peace and blessings of Allah be upon him) is a legislator for mankind, whereas we obey him in all he orders and avoid everything that he prohibits. Allah says, "Or have they partners with Allah who have instituted for them a religion which Allah has not allowed." [41] Ibn Taymiyyah (may Allah have mercy upon him) explained, "Whoever raises and appoints any person then makes loyalty and enmity based on the accord of that person is described in the verse in Ar-Rum, 32."[42] Sheikh Al-Islam (may Allah have mercy upon him) also said, "None one has the right to summon others to a statement or belief that something is correct because of the person who said it. Moreover, Muslims must not fight against other Muslims based on a particular scholar's statement. Rather, when Allah and His Messenger order something, we summon others to follow it because that's obedience to Allah and His Messenger." [43]

The unprincipled, miscreant agenda of propagandists is catalyzed by the reckless abandonment of sincerity due to an unquenchable thirst for dominance. In their breasts fester a lack of sound knowledge, an unhealthy loathing of competition, and a despicably low sense of integrity. Propaganda undermines trust in the source of info and instigates rumor, which can result in the denial of truth when presented. Its insidious affect reaps pessimistic attitudes, encourages violence, and limits the mind's options. Ar-Rahman has taught man to articulate eloquently, a blessing to which propagandists show ingratitude through failure to convey clear truth in an endearing manner that is free from ulterior motive or criminal intent.

Spubs' pompous, self-appointed ministry incorporates a sufi-styled exaltation of its scholars, the scathing defamation of Ahlus-Sunnah, and deception perpetrated by the Shiite, as well as covert accusations of apostasy reminiscent of Khawarij tendencies. They've inseminated the minds of their audience with a pyretic, blind allegiance to their party's protocol, which lacks consistency with their alleged adherence to pure Islamic teaching.

Brainwashing evangelism derails the cognitive senses until one is left wandering and animalistic. The Quran in turn heightens awareness, so in order to gain a sense of direction one must be cultivated upon its pure rudimentary and sophisticated teachings until adorned with piety, intellect, and immune to deceit. Allah asserts, "Oh you who believe, if you fear Allah He will grant you the ability to distinguish between right and wrong." May our shortcomings escort us to sincere repentance, and I invoke Allah to grant us faith that exceeds perpetrating surface belief, conscious discernment, and valor in the face of adversity.

Was-Salaam

The poor servant in need of Allah's mercy

Your Brother,

Abu Aaliyah Ibn Dwight Battle

References:

[1] Collected by Al-Bukhari[6133] and Muslim[2998]

[2] Fathul Bari [10/529] by Ibn Hajr

[3] 'Allamu Us-Sunnan 2/498

[4] Read more: http://www.businessdictionary.com/definition /propaganda.html#ixzz3FO87JfA

[5] Al-'Araf 21-24

[6] Al-Mulk 67:14

[7] Al-Khaf 18:54

[8] Al-Hijr 15: 6

[9] Ad-Dhariyat 51; 52

[10] Al-Hujurat 49; 11

[11] Collected Al-Bukhari [48] and Muslim [64]

[12] https://www.youtube.com/watch?v=3x1xIsqR9 AA or @AbuIyaadSP [tweets] if further evidence is required please email.me @ lamontbattlejr@gmail.com. I'm referring to the TROID & SP Franchise admin as a whole who employ this tactic.

[13] Al-Ahzab 33:69

[14] Collected by Al-Bukhari [3404]

[15] Collected   by   Al-Bukhari[5144]   and Muslim[4917]

[16] Majmu-ul-Fatawa [4/28]

[17] Madarajus Salikin [3/199]

[18] An-Nur 24:15

[19] Explanation of Hadith ul-Ifk, Abdul Ghani Al-Maqdasi page 83

[20]   http://www.islaam.ca/index.php/converts/n-america/333-raha-batts

[21] http://mtws.posthaven.com/shaykh-khaalid-uthman-ibn-dwight-battle-has-not-right-to-use-the-speech-of-the-scholars-to-accuse-the-salafees-of-hizbiyyah

[22] Al-Jami fil Hadith [128] , Abdullah ibn Wahab[d.197H]

[23] I'lam-ul-Muwaqqi-in [6/154]

[24] Al-Baqarah 2:42

[25] Al-Baqarah 2:77

[26] Dar'u al-Ta'arudh al-'Aql wa al-Naql [7/ 170-171]

[27] Al-Munafiqun 63:4

[28] An-Najm 53: 32

[29] Shaykh-ul-Islām Ibn Taymiyyah: Many people test these groups based on suspicion and desires, thus they place their group and those who affiliate with their followers and support them as being among Ahlus-Sunnah. On the other hand everyone who opposes them is considered Ahl-ul-Bid'ah [Majmū' al-Fatāwā [3/346-347].

[30] Al-Ma'odah 5: 18

[31] Fathul Rahman fi Tafsir-Ul Quran, Mujir-ud-deen ibn Muhammad Al-Maqdasi[d927H]

[32] Zaw'id Masa'il-il-Jahiliyah, pg 966

[33] An-Nisa 4: 49

[34] Al-Jami li Ahkam-il-Quran 17/110

[35] Ali-Imran 3:188

[36] Al-Baqarah 2:67

[37] Akhbar-Ul-Hamaq wal-Mughafilin, Ibn Jawzi , pg 25

[38] Az-Zumar 39: 36

[39] Taqdis-al-Ashkhas fi Fikris Sufi [2/193]

[40] https://soundcloud.com/abumiftah/abu-muhammad-warns-from-abu

[41] Ash-Shura 42:21

[42] Hukuml Intimaa ilaa Al-Firaq Wal-Ahzab, Sh Bakr Abu Zayd pg 104-105.

[43] Fatawa Al-Iraqiyah Vol1/ 91-92, Ibn Taymiyyah

Glossary of Propaganda Terms used the Neo Salafy Cult

Character Assassination: the malicious and unjustified harming of a person's good reputation.

Name Calling: abusive language or insults utilized to defame an individual, group, or institution.

Testimonial: the endorsement a product, group, or institution by a well-known public figure.

Bandwagon: an attempt to persuade a target audience to join in and pursue the course of action that seemingly the majority has chosen.

Transfer (Honor by Association): the technique of projecting positive (praise or blame) of a person, entity, object, or value (an individual, group, organization) to another in order to make the second more acceptable.

Invoking the Righteous Call: A person who believes that they are superior to others (and thus deserve favored status) because of their intellect, social status, wealth, or other factors.

Disparaging Education: The lack of reverence for education and intellectualism.

Cherry Picking/Selective Reporting: suppressing evidence or the fallacy of incomplete evidence is the act of pointing to individual cases or data that seem to confirm a particular position, while ignoring a significant portion of related cases or data that may contradict that position.

Rumors and Gossip: Information, ideas, or lies deliberately spread to help or harm a person, group, movement, institution and nation.

Sensationalism: the use of exciting or shocking stories or language at the expense of accuracy, in order to provoke public interest or excitement.

Verdicts by Association: A fallacy that tangles the process of fairly evaluating an idea, person, or group by interjecting irrelevant and misleading negative material. This practice tries to connect beliefs or persons to something unsavory or untrustworthy in order to discredit them.

Culture/ Climate of Fear: is a term used by some scholars, writers, journalists and politicians who believe that some in society incite fear in the general public to achieve political goals

Yellow Journalism: journalism that is based upon sensationalism and crude exaggeration.

Cult of Personality: arises when an individual uses mass media, propaganda, or other methods, to create an idealized, heroic, and at times, worshipful image,often through unquestioning flattery and praise.

Spinning Stories: a form of propaganda, achieved through providing an interpretation of an event or campaign to persuade public opinion in favor or against a certain organization or public figure.

Essay 3- The Extremist Commonality of Takfir and Tabdee
A Glance at the Belief System

Ibn Abbass said: "There will come a group of people who will not understand the Quran the way we do." [Bidiyah wa Nihiya 7/293]

The most dangerous thing to man is when he believes something harmful is good and does evil thinking his deeds are righteous. Allah said: Say "Shall We tell you the greatest losers in respect of (their) deeds "Those whose efforts have been wasted in this life while they thought that they were acquiring good by their deeds![1]

When considering the actions from ISIS, Al-Qa'idah and those extreme in Tabdee, the corruption they have caused to the Muslims in their worship, their intellects and in their family's life, all in the name of Jihad against disbelievers and innovators is evident. As time passes by, it becomes more depressing. These fanatics have no regard for the quality of life and the family structure, and will do anything to destroy a civilized society and divide a family household for the sake of the understanding of their own beliefs.

Reducing the spread of these ideas is the goal if extremism is to be curbed, not necessarily the persons involved. Our concern to protect our religion and family is the primary objective against a cyber-world where ideologues are constantly spreading their beliefs to others. The extremist in Takfir and Tabdee are young self-righteous people who have gone too far. The Prophet (ﷺ) said, "In the last days (of the world) there will appear young people with foolish thoughts and ideas.[2] These adolescents only have a surface knowledge of Islam with a very limited understanding of the Quran and the Sunnah and generally think that they know the truth; and no one else does.

Takfir and Tabdee are legitimate laws in the Islam that must only be applied by scholars well-grounded in the Shar'iah, otherwise when practiced by unqualified and inexperienced people, a grave tragedy will result. The extremist in both of these areas takes a general description for a statement, or an action for one to become an apostate, or innovator and then apply it to specific people without considering the establishment of proof first against that person.

Shaykh Muhammad Bazmoul said: The argument of proof must be given to a Muslim first before he can be considered a disbeliever, an innovator, or a sinner. Allah said: And We never punish until We have sent a Messenger (to give warning)[3].

To say certain speech, actions and beliefs are acts of disbelief and Bi'dah doesn't require the proof to be established, but to apply the ruling of these things to specific people does.[4]

Ibn Taymiyyah said: "No one has the right to take a Muslim out of the realm of Islam through an error or mistake he's made until the proof has been established against him.[5]

Chapter 1: The Unjust application of removing Muslims from Islam and Sunnah

To begin one of the fairly common traits shared with ISIS, Al-Qa'idah and Ahl Tabdee is their inability to distinguish between Takfir and Tabdee in description, in general and specifically. Therefore, if there is any act they perceive as Kufr or Bid'ah, then the ruling applies to that person automatically to be a Kafir or an innovator.

Shaykh Abdullah ibn Muhammad ibn Abdil Wahhab said: "The difference between general and specific is crystal clear; Takfir in general is to declare all people disbelievers whether they know, or don't; and for those whom the proof has been established against, or not. The Takfir in the specific case is for the one who the proof has been given to about the actions of disbelief. [6]

Likewise, Ahl Tabdee take the general text and apply it to any and every one not with them. Shaykh Rabee said: They declare anyone who falls in Bid'ah to be an innovator and they believe Ibn Hajr is more dangerous than Sayyid Qutb .[7]

Imam Al-Albani said: "Everyone who falls into bid'ah isn't an innovator."

Uniquely, the people extreme in Tabdee have their own personal stockpile armory of narrations which they fire at every person who doesn't agree with them. Unlike the Khawarij, who rely on a twisted understanding of the Quran. Ahl Tabdee will say things from Imam Al-Barbaharee's book: Whoever abandons the Jumu'ah or congregational prayer in the mosque, without an excuse, is an innovator."

Consequently, since their masjids in their circles are the only ones where prayer should be offered, they will abandon giving Salams to any and every one that doesn't pray in them.

Shaykh Ahmed An-Najmee commented on Imam Al-Barbaharee' point," If a person doesn't pray in congregation he's sinner or hypocrite, but not an innovator until he stops praying in congregation and Friday prayer believing that the Imam mustn't be followed, but he still isn't considered an innovator.[8]

Imam Ahmed An-Najmee's speech applies to them more than anyone else, as they are known to walk and drive pass every masjid not on the list.

The list could go on and on and the narrations of Salaf aren't proofs for verdicts, unless there is a consensus among them on a particular issue. Otherwise, it's an opinion, and in some instances for a certain period of time in a particular place.

To remedy this problem is easy. Allah said: So ask of those who know the Scripture if you don't.[9] It's not permissible for an ignorant or self-taught individual who puts himself forward to speak about the affairs of the religion without knowledge. Here, it must be reiterated that at the time of questioning a scholar for the verdict about a person that the full name must be mentioned, before any Sheikh's answer can be applied to him in specific. For example, on YouTube you'll find Sheikh Such and Such refutes this one and that one; however, the person's name wasn't mentioned in the question. Accordingly, for that reason, today we need to disregard and stop attributing a scholar's speech to people he didn't intend. This scheme is one often employed by Ahl Takfir and Ahl Tabdee.[10]

Chapter 2 : The belief that anyone who doesn't boycott an innovator should be boycotted[11]

Another similar trait among both fanatics share is whoever doesn't agree with them in Takfir or Tabdee on an individual shares the same ruling. The people of Takfir say whoever doesn't consider a Kafir to be a disbeliever is a Kafir and Ahl Tabdee practice whoever doesn't call such and such an innovator is a person of Bid'ah.[12]

For instance, Ahl Tabdee will say what's your opinion of so and so, and if this person is labeled and you don't agree, then you're forced to wear the same, while others in their more extreme approach will merely just assume you know this person has been called an innovator by one or two, so you must follow suit, otherwise you are defiant. They act this way towards everyone without restriction, it doesn't matter if the issue is unclear or incomprehensible for his fellow Muslim. And to add insult to injury if the person asks for proof, then he's automatically shunned, followed by the boycott. And Allah is a witness of their terror. Allah said: What thing is the greatest in witness?" Say: "Allah (the Most Great!) is Witness between me and you.[13]

Chapter 3: Testing non-members with their leaders

The agreement or disagreement with the zealots of Takir and Tabdee is a mannerism between them and they don't recognize its catastrophe. The believers of Takfir and Tabdee are testing the global population with speeches and actions that are nowhere legislated in Islam, or anywhere in the Shariah. And consequently, have caused bloodshed and turmoil around the globe that only Allah knows to what extent. The Khawarij killed the Prophet's (ﷺ) companion Abullah ibn Khabab. They asked him: What do you say about Abu Bakr and Umar? Abdullah praised them.

Then they asked him: What do you say about the rule of Uthman from the beginning of his government. Abdullah replied he was in right from beginning until the end.

Then they asked him: What's your opinion about Ali before and after his rulership? Abdullah ibn Khabab said: He's more knowledgeable about Allah than you are, and more God-fearing with more insight.

At that moment the Khawarji told him: You follow your desires and support people because of their names and not their actions. I swear to God, we are going to kill you in a way that we haven't killed anyone before.[14]

The extremist of Tadee use their leaders such Abu Khadeejah, Abu Hakeem,Amjad Rafiq and Abul Hasan Malik to determine if a person is a Sunni Muslim. Please refer to Anwar Wright's declaration below which reads, "If you see someone loving Abu Khadeejah, Abu Hakeem,Amjad Rafiq , Abul Hasan Malik then know they are inshallah a person of the Sunnah."[15]

His words are clear and require no explanation.

Shaykh. Ihsan Thahir (1407H) said:

"A cultist invites to his cult and party and orders people to follow men whom Allah hasn't authorized to be followed "

Some of the more extreme followers of Salafi Publications believe that we will be asked about them and Shaykh Rabee in our graves.

Shaykh Rabee Al-Madkhali was asked if it's permissible to make allegiance and disassociation based on specific people? He answered : This spreads the Ghulu(fanaticism)that Allah fights. He said: O people of the Scripture (Jews and Christians)! Do not exceed the limits in your religion, nor say of Allah aught but the truth. The Messiah 'Iesa (Jesus), son of Maryam (Mary), was (no more than) a Messenger of Allah[Fatawa vol1/333]

Chapter 4: The belief that it's permissible to physically and emotionally abuse non-members

The fanatics of declaring Sunni Muslims as innovators will not go to the extreme of killing one who doesn't agree with them, but will harm and have in past physically harmed another Muslim. Sheikh Rabee ibn Hadi Al-Madhkhali said: "They are known by their foul language, harshness, and intimidation of others, to the point they threaten Muslims by physical harm, in fact some of them have actually assaulted other Muslims."[16]

On September 2nd,2016, a message was sent out from a branch of Salafi Publications at Masjid Bin Baz(East London) by Abu Umar Farooq, warning people from speaking about Abu Khadeejah and Bilal Davis(May Allah bless them) and threatening to hunt down anyone who does. He said: Don't speak about them, and Don't refute them, and Don't warn against these individuals, Don't! And those that know of them give them my message. Don't speak about them. Don't speak about the noble brothers. And I'm going to say this every lesson cause I fear that some of them may be in our ranks...We'll hunt them down! That's how it is we'll hunt you down!"[17]

Allah said: It is only Shaitan that suggests to you the fear of his Auliya' [supporters and friends (polytheists, disbelievers in the Oneness of Allah and in His Messenger, Muhammad], so fear them not, but fear Me, if you are (true) believers.[Al-Imran-175] It's Allah the most High Alone who strikes fear in the Hearts of people so, no one is allowed in Islam assume the role of God to use fear against Muslims and humanity. Allah said: We shall cast terror into the hearts of those who disbelieve, because they joined others in worship with Allah, for which He had sent no authority; their abode will be the Fire and how evil is the abode of the Zalimun (polytheists and wrong-doers). [Al-Imran 151]

Previously, similar terroristic threats were issued on the Minbar from two Salafi Masjids under the umbrella of Salafi publications in North America, and through their teachers in Madinah during a phone conversation.[18]

The Messenger of Allah (peace and blessings of Allah be upon him) said, "It is not permissible to spill the blood of a Muslim except in three [instances]: the married person who commits adultery, a life for a life, and the one who forsakes his religion and separates from the community."

Unless they consider speech about Salafi publications an act of apostasy or separation from the community then why issue a direct terroristic threat to Muslims by forbidding things Allah and His Messenger (ﷺ) have made Halal? These kinds of transgressions go unchecked within the circles of the extremists.

A warning for any zealous youth who might think about carrying out his threat against his brother, The Prophet,[ﷺ], "Abusing a Muslim is Fusuq (evil doing) and fighting him is Kufr (disbelief),[19]. Moreover, The Messenger of Allah (ﷺ) said, "Verily your blood, your property and your honor are as sacred and inviolable as the sanctity of this day of yours, in this month of yours and in this town of yours. Verily! I have conveyed this message to you."[20]

It's worth mentioning here that the call of Muhammad ibn Abdil Wahhab doesn't promote terrorism, or sanction attacks against anyone who doesn't agree with them. The Muslim mustn't fight for the sake of one agreeing or disagreeing with his group.[21]

Chapter 5: Marriage with non-members

Another similar belief ISIS, ISIL and the extremists in Tadbee share is they believe that a marriage to a person who doesn't agree with them isn't allowed. This practice of the Khawarij was inherited from the Al-Azariq sect of renegades.[22] Similarly, if a woman complains to some of the fanatics of Tabdee about her husband disagreeing with them, attending classes, or listening to the audios of people they consider astray and off track, then they will promptly assist her with a Khula process as witnessed in the past in Birmingham and presently today among a group known as The Western Salafis of Riyadh ,and in other parts of the world.

Unfortunately, no consideration is given to the welfare of the children; where and with which parent they will stay with after the divorce. Rarely, is the issue of reconciliation encouraged between spouses and at times once the marriage is dissolved does the father stay in touch with his children. Moreover, the fact that some of them are in foreign lands which require a woman's legitimate stay under the sponsorship of her husband isn't studied thoroughly. Nonetheless, our Muslim sisters caught up in this cult's web of deceit are being taken advantage of; some are even remarried for short periods to someone within the crew, and then left stranded with her children. Don't you find it quite convenient that some of the brothers you go to for counseling end up with your ex-wife after your divorce?

There is a consensus among the people of the Sunnah that sins and disobedience don't take a Muslim out of the fold of Islam. Therefore, their marriage remains legal under Islamic law unless it's proven that one of the spouses has truly gone apostate. My advice to all Muslim brothers and sisters is to seek counsel from true Islamic Scholars for their issues of marriage and go to the Islamic courts if you are in Muslim countries. Sideline all people who have a chronic history of serial marriages as a counselor for your situation ;and whoever and wherever you decide to remarry, be sure to have a blood test done for your own safety.

Chapter 6: The belief that all innovation and all innovators are all the same

These radical groups of today are unaware of the complexities in Islam regarding various issues. They don't have a deep understanding of the different kinds of Kufr & Bid'ah and other complex scenarios and their solutions. Limited knowledge is quite dangerous, and it has proved so in today's world. To the extremists of Takfir, Kufr is one and there is no such thing of major and minor. When they see an act mentioned in the general sense that whoever does this is a disbeliever, they then run with it and make Takfir. For instance,"

Allah said: And whosoever does not judge by what Allah has revealed, such are the Kafirun .[Al-Ma'idah :44]

The Kufr in this ayah is one that doesn't take a person out of Islam as explained by Ibn Abbass.

Likewise, the rebels of Tabdee are unable to grasp that all bid'ah is not the same. There are some which are the major ones which take a person out of Islam and others which are minor that don't. There's a difference in the way a caller to Bid'ah is dealt with compared to someone whose Bid'ah is only with himself.

The people extreme in Tabdee don't believe it's allowed for them ask Allah to show mercy on a person of innovation. Shaykh Rabee said: It's permissible to ask Allah to show mercy to the people of innovation and this is the way of the Salaf.

Therefore, they rarely, if ever, make Dua for the Muslims' not with them to be blessed and forgiven.

Chapter 7: The belief that it's permissible to spy on Muslims

The Prophet (ﷺ) said, "Beware of suspicion, for suspicion is the worst of false tales; and do not look for the others' faults and do not spy, and do not be jealous of one another, and do not desert (cut your relation with) one another, and do not hate one another; and O Allah's worshipers! Be brothers (as Allah has ordered you!" [23]

ISIS/Al-Qa'idah generally join social media to keep tabs on the latest visits of Muslim leaders (May Allah strengthen them) around with the World. As soon as they can find a picture of a Muslim ruler with a non-Muslim, they spread it confidentially among themselves using slander, defamation and Takfir.

This is the problem with social media accounts today like Facebook, Youtube and Twitter. All outlets where people have the freedom of speech to say whatever without thought ,or precaution. The best advice about Social media and in particular Twitter was given by the Mufti of Saudi Arabia and translated by our Brother Moosa Richardson of Bakkah.net [24]

The Mufti said about Twitter: Those with no experience or knowledge go on and write whatever they want, follow whomever they want, criticize whomever they want, support whomever they want, and condemn whomever they want, without contemplating or following any Islamic guidelines. Instead, they (Twitter accounts) are websites where people of no specialization or knowledge speak."

The Mufti added: It is a medium of negativity for whirling whimsical insults and baseless personal attacks. These are serious affairs that Muslims are not allowed to be involved in!

Allahu Akbar, and who says the scholars are unaware of what's going! Let's look at an example of what the Mufti of Saudi Arabia is saying so that the picture is clear and the relationship is understood of how both extreme groups act alike and operate to spread their hatred for Muslims who aren't in their group or disagree with them.

A questioner asked me for clarity about the hadith of 73 sects and its authenticity. I tweeted back at him on August 31st,2016 "It's authentic and one of Salafi Imams wrote and entire book explaining the Hadith. this book by Shaykh Abdul Qahir details the Hadith and goes into the sects and what does الأمة mean."

There it is right there. The opportunity for the student of nearly two decades in Saudi at the feet of well-known scholars to attack on my honor, slander me and earn some laughs and retweets. Allah said: If a good befalls you, it grieves them, but if some evil overtakes you, they rejoice at it.[25]

The comical yet sinister thing about this all is, I was blocked from him on Twitter after presenting a knowledge-based theory argument for his feedback, something we both have an email history of over the years. Nevertheless, times have changed and the lines have been drawn in the sands. Let's pause here for a second, and ask ourselves by the way what kind of person blocks someone on Twitter, but then still follows his conversations with others?! Now let's, proceed by looking at his clandestinely written Tweet hidden from my view.

On September 1st,2016 from Moosa Richardson @1MMeducation. "Well-known Ash'aree Abdul-Qaahir al-Baghdadi (d.429) is a "Salafi imam" (!!) to ignorant degree-purchasing frauds." And "The book he introduces as the work of a "Salafi imam" (!!) promotes the deviant Ash'aree Cult as the correct creed of Ahlus-Sunnah! جهل مركب [Compound ignorance]"[26]

He went totally against the advice he himself translated and displayed on Bakkah.net.

Allah said: Enjoin you Al-Birr (piety and righteousness and each and every act of obedience to Allah) on the people and you forget (to practise it) yourselves, while you recite the Scripture]! Have you then no sense? [Al-Baqarah:44]

The Mufti said: Helpful criticism and good advice has its place and channels, and it has its manners. It is not to be spread about on this medium (Twitter) so that people join the bandwagon with lies, fabrications, fraudulence, and personal attacks, casting doubt on many (good) things, calling to confusion, chaos, and every harmful thing.

Imam Al-Barbaharee said: Whoever hides sincere advice from the Muslims has acted deceitfully towards them, so it is not permissible to hide sincere advice from any of the Muslims, whether pious or impious, in matters of the religion. Whoever hides that has acted deceitfully towards the Muslims. Whoever acts deceitfully towards the Muslims has done so towards the religion. Whoever acts deceitfully towards the religion has behaved treacherously towards Allah, His Messenger and the Believers. [27]

Being that he has my email, he could have written to me and discussed the issue like he previously has done in past. Was I wrong for following the praises of Imam As-Saboonee and Imam Ath-Thahabi in Siyr about Abdul Qahir Al-Baghdadee [429H] ?

If I am inviting others to read an Asha'ri leader's book that promotes deviancy then what did Sheikh Zayd Madkhali (Rahimahullah) do by encouraging people to read the book, and the Lajnah of KSA for senior scholars by referencing the book ? [28]

The claim "degree-purchasing frauds". I'll see him in front of Allah with this and for that I say "JazakAllahu khayran."

Allah said: (Remember!) that the two receivers (recording angels) receive (each human being after he or she has attained the age of puberty), one sitting on the right and one on the left (to note his or her actions)… Not a word does he (or she) utter, but there is a watcher by him ready (to record it).

Chapter 8: The belief that advice is withheld from the Muslims they target.

Shaykh Rabee was asked about warning about a man before giving him advice. The Shaykh said: If his evil is imminent, hasten to advise him, this serves the situation better. If he accepts it then good, otherwise warn against him. On the other hand, if his Bid'ah is insignificant then don't make it difficult for him by refuting him publicly.[29]

In a nutshell, extreme groups take a position about a person first, then hold that belief and next label him as unclear. The minute that individual makes a mistake they refute that error publicly. Allah said: but if a calamity overtakes you, they say: "We took our precaution beforehand," and they turn away rejoicing.[30]

Extreme groups don't believe in giving advice to their fellow Muslim. They derive pleasure from picking on others and name-calling to keep their followers eating others' flesh with one-sided propaganda – a more preferred way to travel to their grave; instead of guiding and giving helpful advice to their Muslim brothers.

The Messenger of Allah (ﷺ) said: "Religion is sincerity, religion is sincerity (Al-Nasihah), and religion is sincerity." The followers inquired: "To whom, O Messenger of Allah?" He (ﷺ) replied: "To Allah, to His Book, to His Messenger, to the imams of the Muslims and to their common folk." Only well-intentioned people are sincere enough to provide useful and true advice. The Prophet (ﷺ) said, "None of you become a true believer until he likes for his brother what he likes for himself"

Shaykh Rabee Al-Madkhali said: If your brother falls into an error advise him politely with proof and evidence and Allah will allow him to benefit by using this method. Don't sit and wait until he makes a mistake then spread all over the place, saying So and So did this and that. This approach is the way of the Devil and not the Salaf.[Bahjatul Qari/page 107]

Chapter 9: They name themselves the Saved SECT

The Khawarij have a history of naming themselves in a way of a Tazkiyah. They call themselves Ahlul Iman (the people of faith) and everyone who opposes them they call them Kuffar(Disbelievers) Ibn Taymiyyah said: The people of innovation name themselves with titles they don't deserve, similarly to the way the Khawarij call themselves, "The believers"[31]

The extremists of Tabdee believe they alone are the saved sect and no one else, if you were to ask them or their leaders to name one person who's Salafi in the West that's not with them they probably would avoid answering you or reply with the block button on Twitter.

Shaykh Al-Islam Ibn Taymiyyah said: "The first people to go astray in this area were the Khawarij who considered themselves to be the only ones adhering to the Quran and the Sunnah properly. [32]

The fanatics of removing Muslims from Sunnah have taken the title of Salafiyah and changed it from its original and intended meaning used by the Salaf and scholars to a name brand label advertising their presence. For example, they exploit the word "salafi "only calling themselves, [The Salafis]. This high-minded attitude of theirs has exposed their faith by the way they use the word for practically any and everything they touch, [Salafi products], [Salafi

Eids] and so much more and Allah's refuge is sought.

I ask you, what makes a product Salafi and what is a Salafi Eid again?[33]

Chapter 10: The practice of declaring those closest of kin deviants

This age-old practice among those in extreme is inherited from the Khawarij. They declare their closest relatives apostates, including their mothers and fathers. At-Tabari mentioned that Al-Azraq was a Sunni and when he died his son Naf'I didn't attend his funeral.

The rebels of Tabdee won't attend the funeral any person they consider an innovator, regardless if he is a layman, or ignorant; as their methodology is built on declaring Muslims innovators.

Ibn Taymiyyah said: "It's allowed to ask Allah's Forgiveness for every Muslim that isn't known to be a hypocrite and pray at his funeral, even if he's known to be an innovator, or sinner. However it's not an obligation for every Muslim to attend the funeral."[34]

From the many correspondences I've had with brothers worldwide, I encountered a British brother who grieves severely from not attending his mother's funeral on account that he labeled her an innovator.

Chapter 11: They fight and dispute over issues that scholars differ with.

The Khawarij are known to fight and dispute those who disagree with them in issues that scholars of the past differed over and are unwilling to make an excuse for the person who doesn't side with their view.

Shaykh Al-Islam Ibn Taymiyyah said: This is the reality of the people of innovation and oppression like the Khawariji and other groups. They oppress the Ummah and transgress against those who don't agree with them in issues.[35]

The fanatics of Tabdee in most cases are Hanbalis in their Fiqh, consequently if someone comes with an issue that goes against what their scholars say about the topic, they get angry, or if the person quotes one scholar, they will quote theirs and continue to quote them; as if they are the proof and alone know the truth.

The reason why they quote their scholars with such passion is because they are attached to their personalities more than the Prophet. Consequently you'll notice they quote their scholars position on an issue and then they tag it with the phrase, " We are on the Minhaj of shaykh so and so "

Imam Al-Ghazali, "The nature of weak-minded people is to recognize the truth by the person who said it and not the truth as it is."

Chapter 12: The belief that Senior Salafi Scholars who don't agree with them have issues.

It's almost impossible to hear a praise or recommendation for a Salafy scholar who doesn't agree them. They mainly target the senior scholars in this area. They say things like, "I'm not a fan of Fawzan" "Shaykh Al-Albani and Al-Uthaymeen didn't really understand Minhaj "or their most recent one, "We are waiting for Shaykh Abdul Muhsin to die so that we can warn against his son,"

Additionally, we need to add to the list the statement from Abu Khadeejah: " Sh Rabi, Sh Ubayd,Sh Muhammad Hadi,Sh Abdullah Bukhari: These are the scholars of Madinah most acquainted with Dawa in the UK/USA."[36]

Honestly brothers and sisters, are you that naïve? When was the last time any one of the four scholars he mentioned present in your cities, or country?

What makes them some much more aware of the realities in the West than the list of scholars who have physically seen and visited the UK/USA in last 5 years? Whose informing them about the Dawah in the West ? Are they reliable people?

Ibn Taymiyyah said : The origin of the Khawarij's misguidance is their belief that the scholars of guidance and Sunnah along with the general Muslim communities have deviated and are now astray."[37]

Usamah bin Laden used to consider all Salafi scholars corrupted who didn't agree with him and advised people to avoid them.[38]

Abu Mus'ab As-Syrian said: The evil of Bin Baz and Al-Uthaymeen is more harmful to this Ummah than the harms of Ibn Abi Dawud in his era.[39]

Chapter 13: The belief that non-affiliate masjids are all places of innovation along with their people.

Jama'tul Takfir wal Hijrah was a Khawarij group started by Ali Isma'il and his brother Abdul Fattah in the prisons of Egypt in 1965. Their belief system was built on their name," The Group of declaring Muslims apostate and migration." Their core beliefs were Muslims became infidels by sinning, and especially if they regularly sinned without repentance. Their view was that if a Muslim ruler is a disbeliever then the same applies for his citizens he governs.Also, they only prayed in the Masajid where their Imams lead prayer; as they considered all other masjids as Darar.[40] In a like manner, the extremists in Tabdee will only pray in what their leaders call a Salafi Masjid, deem everyone who falls into what they perceive as innovation as an innovator, and if a teacher errs then they view that all of his students have shared in the ruling as well. With such similarities shared between these two, we can call the second group (جماعة التبديع و الهجر والعزل)

Sheikh Rabee said if the scholars have proof that a scholar is astray then the verdict for his students can only be applied to those who are affected and in contact with him.[41]

In regards to boycotting people, then the decision is to be made by the scholars, not the Du'at or the layman.

Shaykh Rabee said: The Salaf used to boycott innovators, but this decision must be made by the scholars to determine if it's suitable, or not. Thus if it's better to avoid boycotting him and call his attention to what is correct, and you and him can see eye to eye, then don't end your relationship with him.[42]

Since the Khawarij's methodology is built on Takfir on sinful Muslims and removing Muslims from Islam through actions that don't necessitate that ruling, they believe that everyone who's not with them is a Kafir. Hence the people not in their ranks blood, wealth and honor are all lawful for the taking. Based on this ideology they don't consider the prayer behind a person who opposes them to be acceptable.

Al-Harith ibn Rashid An-Najee revolted against Ali ibn Talib and said: " I swear to God Ali, I won't obey you and I won't pray behind you! Ali replied: You are fool then, if you want to disobey your Lord and break your oath, you are only harming yourself." [43]

The extremist in Tabdee often quote and misunderstand the narrations: " We don't pray behind innovators ", and in their dogma every Muslim not in their club is an innovator, and the fastest way to expose this belief of theirs is to ask them when they say So and So is an innovator, What's his innovation ? What have the Ulema said about him?

Subsequently, by default they abandon prayer behind their estimation of Ahlul Bid'ah. Abullah ibn Ahmed asked his father Imam Ahmed about praying behind the people of Bid'ah and he answered: Don't pray behind those with the belief of Jahmiyah and Mu'tazeelah .

Also Imam Ahmed didn't allow the prayer behind the Rafidha cult.

Muslims regardless of race and gender remain under their "Guilty until proven Innocent" radar until certain allegiances are taken. They misuse Imam Al-Barbaharee's quote: " Today we test people with the Sunnah "

Shaykh Ahmed An-Najmi said :Testing people in order to affirm if they are from Ahlus Sunnah or not ? What's apparent is the general people are following the generalities of Islam and NO ONE should be tested until it shows that his beliefs aren't from the doctrine of Ahlus Sunnah. Then in that case if it appears that he has beliefs of Irja, Al-Jahmiyyah, As-Sufiyyah and Ar-Rafidha, then he's tested with the questions those groups are tested with.

For example : If he's a Murji'a ask him does Iman increase and decrease or if he's a Rafidha ask him if the Ahl Bayt are infallible or not and etc.[44]

Chapter 14: They harm and attack Muslims and leave alone pagans.

The Prophet (ﷺ) said: They will kill the Muslims but will not disturb the idolaters.

This is among the most witnessed distinct trait of the Khawariji. In the same token the extremists of Tabdee remain silent against modern movements of innovations such as the Muslim LGBT, Muslim feminist cults and so forth, yet praise leaders like Barack Obama and David Cameron; both pushing those agendas. Praising the Kuffar gives them the sense of satisfaction that their deeds are acceptable and praiseworthy. Allah said: Think not that those who rejoice in what they have done (or brought about), and love to be praised for what they have not done,- think not you that they are rescued from the torment, and for them is a painful torment.[Al-Imran:188]

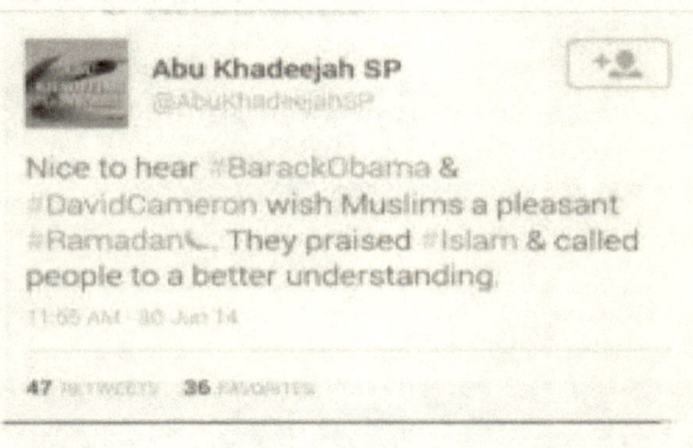

To repeat, their interactions with non-Muslims compared to how they treat Muslims is more widely recognized from their tongues. Their compliments for disbelievers and verbal attacks for Muslims are more frequent in their Dua.

They say things against Muslims like; May Allah burn his face, May Allah allow him die with no one to wash his body, Oh Allah unite him with the Dajjal, May Allah not allow you to die before you tried and troubled with prostitutes, and their favorite one is, "May Allah break your back "

Ibn Qayyim Al-Jawziyyah said: A person's tongue can give you a taste of what's in his heart."

Chapter 15: The Belief that sins doesn't harm Salafiyyah

The Khawarji have the belief that faith is one and doesn't consist of branches, while some fanatics of Tabdee believe the association to Salafiyyah   is the most important thing in this religion no matter what. This is Irja.

The Prophet (ﷺ) said" And whoever is slowed down by his actions, will not be hastened forward by his lineage.

They have a few narrations they rely on to keep their egos high in the faces of their true reality.

Sufyaan ath-Thawree (d. 161H) said: Innovation is more beloved to Iblees than sin, since a sin may be repented from but innovation is not repented from.

Imaam Ahmad said, The graves of Ahl us-Sunnah from those who committed the major sins are like gardens. And the graves of Ahl ul-Bid?ah from amongst their abstemious pious ones are hollow and empty. The sinners of Ahl us-Sunnah are the Awliyaa? (Friends) of Allaah and the abstemious pious ones of Ahl ul-Bid?ah are the Enemies of Allaah.

This narration from Imam Ahmed requires more study and shouldn't be left general to the public as is. For instance, Imam Ahmed is talking about a matter of the unseen that requires revelation. The condition for everyone after their death is unknown to us, except those whom Allah and His Messenger have mentioned.

Allah's Prophet (ﷺ) said: The dead is punished in the grave because of wailing on it.[45]

Once the Prophet (ﷺ) went through the grave-yards of Medina and heard the voices of two humans who were being tortured in their graves. The Prophet (ﷺ) said, "They are being punished, but they are not being punished because of a major sin, yet their sins are great. One of them used not to save himself from (being soiled with) the urine, and the other used to go about with calumnies (Namima)." Then the Prophet asked for a green palm tree leaf and split it into two pieces and placed one piece on each grave, saying, "I hope that their punishment may be abated as long as these pieces of the leaf are not dried."[46]

Moreover, was Imam Ahmed referring to the people of bid'ah in this narration whose Bid'ah takes them out of Islam or what?

When we abandon the primary sources for reference in Islam. i.e Quran, Sunnah and Ijma and rely on secondary sources as our evidences all kinds of confusion and misinterpretations can occur.

Sins can and do affect a person's Aqeedah , actions and can lead to kufr.

The Prophet(ﷺ)said: Bad character ruins deeds the same way vinegar spoils honey.[47]

Shiekh Al-Uthaymeen said: "When a person's manners become bad so does his Aqeedah."

Chapter 16: Conclusion

The most alarming danger posed by people extreme in Takfir and Tabdee is their intolerance. Extremists in Takfir and Tabdee hurt innocent people while believing they are doing righteous deeds with their sense of absolutism. If anyone presents information that's doesn't fit their thought process, it is dismissed no matter how rationally valid it is. These extremists have a sense of knowing the ultimate meaning. They are the most stubborn people you'll even meet with no objectivity. They dehumanize everyone who doesn't agree with them; thus, they feel the power harm and abuse outsiders.

There is no better way anyone can defend the whole world from the cruel acts of ideological terrorism who have harmed thousands of innocent people, than spreading the real and the true teachings of Islam and the Shariah. It is time that we deter this dangerous threat to our world by working together on the wavered minds & ideologies of such people and teach the true message of Islam and Sunnah. As time passes by, this group like every other movement will implode as you are witnessing now, so remain firm and patient and constantly repent to Allah and carry on. As the people they once liaised with in the city of the Prophet are being silenced by the Government through promises of silence, while others are being giving exits permits just look around and you'll notice the echos from the keyboards have almost stopped. And All praises to Allah

Written and prepared by

Abu Aaliyah Abdullah ibn Dwight Battle

The Preachers for Salafi Publications/ Troidca

THE WORLD'S TEST FOR THE ABOVE NAMES ENDORSED/RETWEETED BY SALAFIPUBLICATIONS

Tweet
In reply to @muhiyad
Salafi Pubs and others retweeted
AbooZaahidMeekins
@AbuZaahidMeekins
@muhiyad 4:- if you reside in the United Kingdom test them with @SalafiPubs and those with them in creed.
RETWEETS FAVORITES
Timeline   Notifications   Messages   Me

Tweets
AbooZaahidMeekins
@muhiyad 5:- If you reside in Washington/Baltimore area test them with Kashiff Khan the noble teacher in that area
AbooZaahidMeekins
@muhiyad 4:- if you reside in the United Kingdom test them with @SalafiPubs and those with them in creed.
AbooZaahidMeekins
@muhiyad 3:- If you reside in Canada ask them their connections with the noble brothers of @troidca
AbooZaahidMeekins
@muhiyad 2:- with Abul-Hasan Malik our noble elder and teacher. Or Hasan Somali the noble teacher and imam of
Timeline   Notifications   Messages   Me

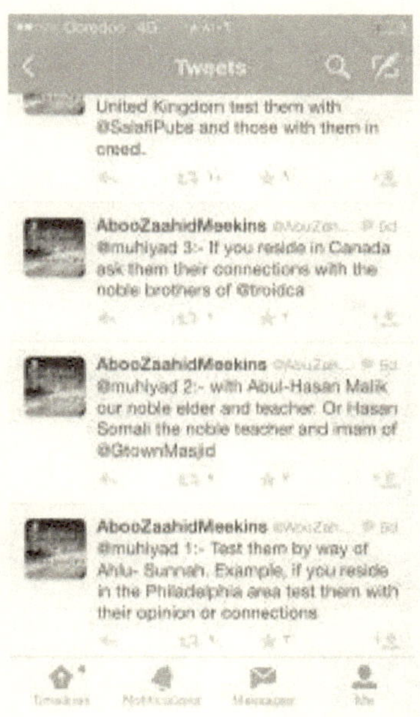

Abu Khadeejah blankets the scholars and Masjids in the UK as Ahl Bid'ah

[1] Quran:Khaf:103

[2] Sahih al-Bukhari 5057

[3] [Al-Isra:15]

[4] Sharh Usul wa Dawabit fee Takfir, by Shaykh Abdul Latif Al-Ash-Shaykh, explained by Shaykh Muhammad Bazmoul.

[5] Majmou 12/501

[6] Majmou/s Rasa'il 1/44/

[7] Minhaj Al-Hadadiyyah.

[8] Irshadus Saree/pg 203/

[9] Quran :16:43

[10] Youtube channels are loaded with this practice.

[11]https://www.abuaaliyah.com/2014/10/17/boycotting-a-person-who-doesnt-boycott-a-deviant/

[12] Taqreer Aa-Imahtu Dawah, Shaykh Muhammad Tahir, page 111

[13] Quran : 6:19

[14] Darur As-Siniyah.

[15]

[16] Minhaj Al-Hadadiyyah, by Al-Alamah, Ash-Shaykh Rabee,point #9

[17] Pay close attention to their words

Abu Umar Faarooq Masjid bin Baz(East London)

[18] Umar Quinn of Masjid Rahmah(Newark NJ):

https://app.box.com/s/4hs7lpbo2hk38bbidsmrrx346gc4lqdy

Abu Hasan Malik (Masjid Muhammad ibn Abdul Wahaab – Camden, New Jersey)

from 17:00 until then end:

complete   audio here https://app.box.com/s/4hs7lpbo2hk38bbidsmrr x346gc4lqdy

Abdul Wali Nelson(Masjid Ad Da'wah Ilat Tawheed Baltimore Md)

:https://www.youtube.com/watch?v=2D6ObwCS9L M

[19] [Al-Bukhari and Muslim].

[20] [Al-Bukhari and Muslim].

[21] Taqreer Al-Aimahtu Dawah, pg 571, Shaykh Muhammad Tahir

[22] IBID

[23] Sahih al-Bukhari 6064

[24] http://www.bakkah.net/en/muftee-saudi-arabia-twitter.htm

[25] Quran :3:120

[26] @1mmeducation on September 1st

,2016 notice how my name is reddened out !

[27] Sharhus Sunnah by Imam Al-Barbaharee

[28] Ajwabatus Sadeedah vol3/429

[29] Fatawa vol1/278

[30] Taubah 50

[31] [Bayyan Talbees/20/135]

[32] [Al-Istaqamah 1/13]

[33] Abu Hasan Malik Al-Akhdar titled his EID SALAFI, perhaps the first in history to do so

[34] Minhaj As-Sunnah/5/235

[35] Majmou 17/311

[36] Quotes like this is why they have been accused of restricting Salafiyyah to only 4. Look at the names often quoted.

[37] Majmou 28/497

[38] Ibn Laden the leader of this era, by Al-Faris Az-Zahrani, pg 401

[39] Death to the Scholars/ by Abu Mus'ab pg 17

[40] Al-Mowsoo'ah Al-Maysar vol1/ 333-338

[41] Fatawa Shaykh Rabee / vol 1/ 343

[42] Fatawa Shaykh Rabee / vol 1/ 278

[43] Bidiyah wan nihiya/7/339 – r

[44] Sharhu Sunnah/ pg 227-228

[45] Sahih Muslim 927
[46] Sahih al-Bukhari 6055

[47] At-Tabarani (12/543) Hasan by Al-Albani

Essay 4- A Dialogue between Abu Thabit and Abul Munaqid

((Unlocking the mind of a Hizbi))*Allah said: Had it been from other than Allah, they would surely have found therein much contradictions.[4:82]*

Abu Thabit: As-Salamu

alaykum Abul Munaqid :

Abu Thabit : As-Salamu alaykum wa

rahmatulilah Abul Munaqid:

Abu Thabit: As-Salamu alaykum wa rahmatulilahi wa Barakatahu

Abul Munaqid:

Abu Thabit: I'm sorry are you

Muslim? Abul Munaqid: I'm Salafi

Abu Thabit : So am I, but you didn't reply to my greetings

Abul Munaqid: I don't give salams to innovators

Abu Thabit : Akhi, are you for real?

Abul Munaqid : The Salaf didn't give salams to innovators

Abu Thabit: Cmon man. What About Ibn Abbass

Abul Munaqid: What about him?

Abu Thabit: When he went to debate the Khawarij he gave them salams first. Is my innovation like that of the Khawarij or worse?

Abul Munaqid: you say you Salafi, but I don't see you pray with the Salafis

Abu Thabit: Is my Salafiyah validated by whether or not I pray with the salafis ?

Abul Munaqid : Im saying though, if you were truly Salafi you'd pray with the Salafis

Abu Thabit: Where do the salafis

pray?

Abul Munaqid In the Salafi Masajid.

Abu Thabit: What makes a masjid Salafi Akhi? What are the conditions?

Abul Munaqid: Look man, at the Salafi masajid, we have Salafi Darus, with the Salafi duat from our elders from the likes of Abu Khadeejah, Abul Hasan Malik, Hasan Somali, and their likes.

Abu Thabit: So you are saying Salafi classes given by Salafi teachers makes a masjid Salafi?

Abul Munaqid: Nah, don't ask me ask the ulema .

Abu Thabit: Akhi Im asking you because you labeled your masjid salaf, so that means I pray with Ahlul bida'?

Abul Munaqid: man the salafi Masajid, have salafi Darus with salafi teachers. I'm saying that's what's going on there.

Abu Thabit: Akhi, I think you are forgetting something, because many masajid around the world fit this condition, like the prophet's masjid, and the Haram in Mecca.

Abul Munaqid: alright.

Abu Thabit: yea, and I don't see the Ulema name those two holiest places in the World as Salaf Masjids. Can you tell me one scholar who said the Haraam and the Prophet's Masjid are Salafi Masjids?

Abul Munaqid: I'll hafta check and get back to you, but I remember the noble brothers posted something from Sheikh Muqbil mentioning Salafi Masjid.

Abu Thabit: What was Imam Muqbil's proof and is the statement of a scholar evidence or a means to understand evidence?

Abul Munaqid: You trying to diss the Sheikh . Imam Muqbil always spoke with Daleel. You don't know?

Abu Thabit: No I am not disrespecting the Shiekh, but I am asking you for his proof to call a masjid Salafi? Can we call an Eid Salafi since Muslims gather there like they do in a masjid? So what's his proof?

Abul Munaqid: I don't know what his proof is? But Im sure he had it.

Abu Thabit: So, you blind following the Sheikh?

Abul Munaqid: So what's wrong with following a scholar?

Abu Thabit : Nothing, but if you are acting by his speech for your actions it's better to know what his proof is. Abu Hanifah said: it's not permissible for anyone to act by my speech unless he knows what my evidence is.

Abul Munaqid: ok, Ill check with the noble ustadz and sms you the dalil or hit you on Facebook.

Abu Thabit: Cool, so do you only pray in Salafi Masjids?

Abul Munaqid: man I bump my head wherever I'm at and the salah comes in.

Abu Thabit: Don't say bump my head, that's not a term for Salah given by the salaf or the Prophet. I gotta question for you. If the all the masajid you pray in are the only Salafi masajid, what about the other masajid that you don't consider Salafi are they places of bidah and its' people?

Abul Munaqid: Akhi, I aint say that.

Abu Thabit: But I'm asking you akhi. You didn't give me salams because you said you don't see me pray with the Salafis and you said you don't give salams to innovators.

Abul Munaqid: Nah, really, I didn't give you salams because you aint clear.

Abu Thabit: clear? am I blurry?

Abul Munaqid: I saw you supporting that conference at Brixton. They support Al- Mara'bi and Al-Halabi. We don't gather and support with people who support and defend deviants with false principles or those who attack Sheikh Rabee the Imam of Jarh wa Ta'dil.

Abu Thabit: Brother, Shiekh Salih As-Suhyamee and Shiekh as-Sindi were going to be there and they dont support Al-Mara'bi or Al-Halabi and corrected someone who spoke ill of Sheikh Rabee at the conference. Is Sheikh As-Suhaymee a Salafi scholar? Can we say Shiekh As-Suhaymee and Sheikh As-Sindi are deviants now because they were at Brixton masjid?

Abul Munaqid: The Ustadz, our elder, the noble brother Abu Khadijah said we don't go and gather with ahlul bida'h this strengthens their numbers.

Abu Thabit: yeah, I remember that audio and Abu Aaliyah said he made blanket Tabdee with that statement.

Abul Munaqid: Man that guy is a pretender, a hater, a degree purchasing fraud, a shameless hip- hop fanatic and a liar. Abu Khadeejah never said all of the scholars who attend the conference are innovators. Your mans need to repent.

Abu Thabit: Wow the name calling goes on well with you. Akhi, perhaps the spinning tactic of this brother has caused you to forget the English language and principles in usul al fiqh.[1]

Abul Munaqid: what are you saying

Abu Thabit: his response was that similar to Ahlul Bida' when they face strong proof. Name –calling. Next point Abu Aaliyah never said that Abu Khadeejah said all the scholars who attend the conference are all innovators, but maybe you and AbuKhaeejah don't know the context of his sentence and his actions. For example, If I say I like apples and oranges and mangoes. Which fruit do I like?

Abul Munaqid: Apple , oranges and mangoes.

Abu Thabit: but Akhi I only said I like apples, so why are you adding oranges and mangoes?

Abul Munaqid: because you said , "and."

Abu Thabit: Tayyib, so now let's listen to his statement again.[2]

Abul Munaqid: ok play the ustadz words.

Abu Thabit : Ok ima pause it here . He acknowledged that people are leaving him, so he's angry. "Every year a corner of the masjid gone." He said it right?

Abul Munaqid: yeah, now play it again.

Abu Thabit: " you don't want the truth go..They say we're going up the road because sheikh fulan is coming, oh we're going down to Luton because sheikh Fulan is coming,oh we're going to Brixton because sheikh Fulan is coming, so you'll gather with ahlil Bid'ah"

Abul Munaqid: ok , so what !

Abu Thabit: Do you understand English? Yes or no?

Abul Munaqid: yes, I'm saying what's wrong with what he said though.

Abu Thabit: did he or did he not say, sheikh fulan is coming, so you'll gather with ahlul bid'ah. Aren't those his words?

Abul Munaqid: yes, but he didn't say all the scholars. Mr. Battle tricking you. He said, so you'll gather with Ahlul bid'a meaning those masjid.

Abu Thabit : Where on the audio did he say those masjid? He clearly said, sheikh fulan is coming after mentioning various masjid then he said, So you'll gather with Ahlil Bid'ah. Whose gathering with Ahil bidah then? If it's the masjids that's intended and not the scholars as you claim, then aren't those scholars who gather at those masjids blameworthy too? Or do they have diplomatic immunity?

Abul Munaqid: I didn't get you,

Abu Thabit: You are trying to interpret his clear speech for his defense, when he clearly said:" shaykh fulan is coming, so you'll gather with ahlul bid'ah" and everyone who understands English will tell you the context of his words means the scholars are included. Next point for the sake of argument you said his intention for his words," gather with Ahlil Bid'ah refers to the masjid. Correct?

Abul Munaqid: yeah

Abu Thabit: so , if those masjids is what's intended when he said Ahlil Bid'ah .

Abul Munaqid: It is. He's referring to those masajid being places of bid'ah

Abu Thabit: Ok then what does that say about the scholars who visit those places and teach there then? Aren't they gathering with Ahlil bid'ah? You say a man is on the religion of his companions!!

Abul Munaqid: I told you Im a layman I can't make a ruling on people. You should ring the Ustadz and the noble elders at SP directly.

Abu Thabit : Akhi , let me be frank with you I prefer to avoid the ustadz for many reasons and among them is the fact that scholars have warned against him and in particular Sheikh Wasiullah Abbass and Sheikh Khalid Ar-Radaddi.[3] And Shaykh Salih As-Suhaymee said he was ignorant.[4]

Abul Munaqid: Sheikh Wasiullah is an Alim and he's wrong about the Maktabah. He only criticized them because of his love with Ahlul hadith and Green lane masjid and other people put some stuff about our noble brothers in the Sheikh's ear. Plus, scholars in madina praise them.

Abu Thabit: AKhi it's a detailed criticism and doesn't it take precedence over a general praise?

Abul Munaqid: Akhi, the elder, the noble brother Abu Khadeejah is a man who calls to the following of the Scholars. What are the people you take from calling to?[5]

Abu Thabit: They call to Allah and the obligation to follow the messenger and not only the opinions of scholars. So Sheikh Wasiuallah sat with the maktabah for hours and asked them for proof and they couldn't produce a shred of evidence and you call this an error?.[6]

Abul Munaqid: ustadz Anwar Wright destroyed the doubts about that criticism. When you have criticism like this you must first look to see if the man is calling to sunnah in his speech and action and that's what our noble elder, our ustdaz does and his trustworthiness is established. Al-Hamdulilah. [7]

Abu Thabit: So you are saying Sheikh Wasiuallah is wrong? and his criticism isn't in detail ? And the sheikh after sitting with them for hours only based his judgment on his desires?

Abul Munaqid : Nah, I aint saying all that but the if you knew the maktabah you'd know the Sheikh is wrong this time, but he still a scholar though. We can accept and reject every scholars statement except the Prophet.

Abu Thabit: So let me ask you this then if Sheik Wasiuallah is wrong about our brother Abu Khadeejah why can't Sheikh Rabee be wrong about Tahir?

Abul Munaqid: Aw you see you trying to defame and drop all the sheikhs' criticisms. You liar, you dajjal, you imbecile you Ahmaq. You trying to attack the sheikh. He's the Imam of Jarh wa Ta'dil. Sheikh Al-Albani said: He flag bearer of Jarh wa Ta'dil.[8]

Abu Thabit: Yo man! Calm down! How did I attack the sheikh? I simply said if sheikh Wasiuallah is wrong about Abu Khadeejah , then why can't Sheikh Rabee be wrong about Tahir? That's all I said!

Abul Munaqid : Naw you playing with words. Ayo, I know what you trying do. Tahir was criticized by Sheikh Rabee

Abu Thabit: Is his criticism general or detailed?

Abul Munaqid: well the Sheikh said if he was salafy he'd write the bayyan and free himself of Mara'bi and Halaby and not write against the salafis.

Abu Thabit: Ok, I'm asking you is that detailed or general? And does not writing a bayyan take a person out of Salafiyyah?[9]

Abul Munaqid: it's a criticism and he shoulda wrote the bayyan

Abu Thabit: Other scholars in his city, madeenah where he's lived since about 96 or 97 advised him not to and said there was no need for it. That's one point, the second point is a person can say the same thing about that criticism you reject against Abu Khadeejah for the criticism of Sheikh Rabee. It was built off erroneous information. Sheikh Suhaymee asked Abu Khadeejah for 1 piece of evidence that he gathered against Sheikh Tahir and he couldn't do it. Not one piece of evidence. [10]

Abul Munqid: you see, you calling him sheikh. You supporting him and Madeenah.con and the likes of those that of which have come with Tamyee'.

Abu Thabit: no, I'm calling him Sheikh because scholars in madinah call him sheikh. Scholars like Ali Nasir Al-Faqeeh, Sheikh As-Suhyamee and Sheikh Abdur Razzaq . At his Masters dissertation Sheikh Abdur Razzaq actually said that Shiekh Tahir was among their status now before bursting into tears. So now I ask you what do you do when you have a detailed praise and a general criticism. Not to mention Shiekh Tahir lives in Madeenah and Sheikh Rabee at that time lived in Mecca. So could it be possible that the scholars in madeenah who see him every day were more familiar with him more than Sheikh Rabee was?

Abul Munaqid: What you saying Sheikh Rabee is ignorant? He bases his criticisms off proofs and evidences.

Abu Thabit: No, Im not saying he's ignorant, but I am saying he's not infallible.

Abul Munaqid: Yeah, I hear you.

Abu Thabit: ok check this out, what was it that made sheikh Rabee come to his conclusion? Did he go through sheikh Tahir lectures or visit Madeenah.com website? What was it the evidence?

Abul Munaqid: you trying to dispraise the sheikh, you are a fool, you all caught up in the MADCON fitnah. You support the likes of those clowns and their games.

Abu Thabit: Akhi watch the name calling and how am I dispraising the sheikh? Ok, take this then, can I marry you daughter without a wali ?

Abul Munaqid: No- the hadith says the marriage without a wali is invalid.

Abu Thabit: Is Abu Hanifah an Imam from Ahlus Sunnah?

Abul Munaqid: yes of course

Abu Thabit: Well, his view is a woman doesn't need a wali.

Abul Munaqid: He's wrong

Abu Thabit: what about gold for women, is it halal of Haraam?

Abul Munaqid: Gold is Haram for men to wear but Halal for women

Abu Thabit: Sheikh Al-Albani considered it was Haraam for women as well.

Abul Munaqid: He was wrong.

Abu Thabit: does touching a woman break wudu?

Abul Munaqid: No, the prophet [ﷺ] kissed his wives then went to the prayer.

Abu Thabit: Imam Ash-Shafa'I believed it did

Abul Munaqid : I think He was wrong

Abu Thabit: Alright brother, I just mentioned 3 positions from 3 Imams and you rejected their positions. Why ?

Abul Munaqid: cuz their positions went against the evidence.

Abu Thabit: So if a scholar goes against the evidence we can reject his position

Abul Munaqid: yeah

Abu Thabit: I noticed you didn't call me names and you didn't raise your voice and express the same zeal for Abu Hanifa, Al-Albani and Ash-Shafa'I . Like you did for sheikh Rabee.

Abul Munaqid: Akhi, Im straight! Ima stick to Spubs. They are our elders in Dawah. The likes of Kashif Khan, Umar Quinn, Hasan Somali, Abul Hasan Malik, Moosa Richardson and others from their likes.

Abu Thabit: Elders, Elders, huh, Akhi none of them are as old as Dawud Abeeb. He's a senior citizen and has been giving Dawah since the 80's. Why didn't you mention his name?

Abul Munaqid: Who is he?

Abu Thabit : He was the Imam on Lincoln street and played a role for introducing Salafiyah to the west way back when.

Abul Munaqid: Oh yeah, I remember now. He got issues.

Abu Thabit: Issues, Is he a deviant?

Abul Munaqid: Man, he lectures with Zahid Rashid at Al-Baseerah, who also didn't write the bayyan and free himself from Halaby and Ma'rabi and their likes.

Abu Thabit: What is wrong with Zahid? He brings scholars here every summer.

Abul Munaqid: Really, I didn't hear about this.

Abu Thabit: that's cuz you isolated in your salafi Masajid. He brought Shiekh Fahad Al-Fuhayd twice and Sheikh Khalid ar-Raddadi once. Are they Salafi or deviants?

Abul Munaqid: Yo look man, I aint gonna make Tabdee of the scholars I leave that for the people of knowledge.

Abu Thabit: Ok, fair enough, but you said Dawud Abeed has issues cause he works with Zahid Rashid but you won't say the same thing for people more knowledgeable than he is, who also work with Zahid. So if Brixton Masjid is deviant, Green Lane

Masjid is deviant, and Zahid has issues, then what does that say about the scholars who visit them? Are they unaware of these organizations and individuals' true nature or are they deviants?

Abul Munaqid: maybe

Abu Thabit: I got it now. You roll with the group that title themselves "The Salafis."

Abul Munaqid: Yes, they are upon clarity in Minhaj and clarity in Salafiyyah and clarity in Aqeedah.

Abu Thabit: Akhi I hate to inform you of this now , but they have characteristics of a cult .[11]

Abul Munaqid: Man go ahead with that. That's that paper that Lamont Shameless printed it was made to attack the noble upright elders of Salafiyyah.

Abu Thabit: How do you figure so, I read the paper, and he didn't mention any names?

Abul Munaqid:

Abu Thabit: Ok, name one person. Just one person they consider and accept as a salafi muslim from the Duat that's not with them?

Abul Munaqid:

Abu Thabit: cmon brother , just one in the west, and stop giving me that deer in the headlight stare.

Abul Munaqib: If those Duat were salafi they'd work with our brothers from the likes of Germantown and Masjid Rahmah.

Abu Thabit: Akhi, so it's a condition to work with those masajid?

Abul Munaqid: Man the Salafis are united. Allahu Akbar.

Abu Thabit: I don't doubt that "The Salafis " are united.

Abul Munaqid: Yep upon clarity in minhaj.

Abu Thabit: you mentioned masjid Rahmah where did the former Imam study at again?

Abul Munaqid: he got understanding and quotes the athar of the salaf.

Abu Thabit : You mentioned Germantown Masjid. How long was Hasan Somali in Yemen for again and what did he study? By the way didn't you hear what happened between him and Abdul Fattah over a Facebook post?

Abul Munaqid: Naw. What happened?

Abu Thabit: khalas Ima let you ask them. But if they don't answer you I'll share the incident and his phone number so you can call him.

Abul Munaqid: Son! It's like you got nothing better to do than to attack the Salafis

Abu Thabit: Attack, no don't say that but rather say criticize. Who is above reproach? I can see you new, so how about you open your eyes, read and ask questions.

Abul Munaqid: No, I am not new; I'm just coming home from prison.

Abu Thabit: good ,fresh start. Get a job, go back to school and focus on the things that benefit you in this life and in the hereafter, don't waste your time with these guys to much.

Abul Munaqid: Yes-Alhamdulilah. I learnt my Salafiyyah inside. We have to avoid the innovators and stay away from the Hizbis like, Ali Davis, Muhammad Muneer, Mr.Battle and their likes.

Abu Thabit: Akhi, watch your tongue . The Angels are recording.

Abul Munaqid: Man, them dudes got Tamyee and support Hizbis, so we group people with their friends. Don't you know the Hadith? "A man follows the religion of his companions and the Salaf used to say whoever hides his bida from us can't hide his companionship.

Abu Thabit: What's wrong with Muhammad Muneer?

Abul Munaqid: He supports Tahir and Madeenah.con and lectures at Siraj Wahhaj Masjid.

Abu Thabit: Ok so the scholars in madeenah deviant too who support Tahir?

Abul Munaqid: man stop bringing the scholars in this. You asked me why Muhammad Muneer is deviant and I told you

Abu Thabit: please! You use an issue that not's connected to the usul of the sunnah, and then join it to those you disagree with to declare them astray and innovators. Madeenah.com, man Sheikh Khalid Ar-Raddadi was a moderator of the site until he stopped due to his work load.

Abul Munaqid: And Ali Davis has ikhwani and Tamyee principles. He on a flyer calling to unity with deviants.

Abu Thabit: it isn't everyone who involves themselves in politics and calls to unity to be called an Ikhwani, unless you think we are supposed to call to separation .It is not permissible to teach a misguided Muslim? Are they going there teaching? Are there any restrictions being placed on them from the host?

Abul Munaqid: You don't know the seerah? The dawah of the Prophet was to call to separation . Don't you know he was sent with suratul -Kafiroon ?

Abu Thabit: naw you got a misunderstanding here and this is getting lengthy plus I got errands to run, but dig this each and every one we spoke about today has articles, audios and books available. PLEASE PRODUCE SOME EVIDENCE THAT GOES AGAINST THE QURAN , OR THE SUNNAH, OR THE IJMA OF THE SALAF BY WAY OF THEIR SPEECH OR WRITINGS. Otherwise ill hafta consider your refutations from you and your group as bogus and fraudulent that are built off of jealously .Ok? As-salamu alaykum

Abul Munaqid:

Abu Thabit: AKhi I gave you salams, we done, As- salamu alaykum

Abul Munaqid:

Abu Thabit: Man never mind, As-salamu alaykum wa Rahmatulilahi wa Barakatahu.. Im out

Allah mentioned the people of innovation and misguidance reject clear proof.

And even if you were to bring to the people of the Scripture (Jews and Christians) all the Ayat (proofs, evidences, verses, lessons, signs, revelations, etc.), they would not follow your Qiblah (prayer direction), nor are you going to follow their Qiblah (2:145).

Prepared by Abu Aaliyah Abdullah ibn Dwight Battle

References:

[1] https://www.youtube.com/watch?v=QUageRm4EAg&index=5&list=PLrym_grlN1V9RyUrWX_ZL_C_979FgBiyY

[2] https://www.youtube.com/watch?v=MraCqmz47zI&index=2&list=PLrym_grlN1V9RyUrWX_ZL_C_979FgBiyY

[3] https://www.youtube.com/watch?v=4y91m87hQPM

[4] https://www.youtube.com/watch?v=7ck6Nj4AQsI&index=3&list=PLrym_grlN1V9RyUrWX_ZL_C_979FgBiyY

[5] Audio:visit www.abuaaliyah.com

[6] https://islam4me.wordpress.com/2011/06/18/the-reason-why-sheikh-waseeallah-abbas-warned-against-abu-khadeejah-salafi-publications-and-their-followers/

[7] https://www.youtube.com/watch?v=qEN8FpkUqL8

[8] This is results from the teaching of Abul Hasan Malik: https://www.youtube.com/watch?v=-wyk7WkxKk0

[9] Shaykh Ubaid Al-Jabiree [may Allah preserve him] said both Shiekhs,Ahmed Bazmoul and Usama Atayah were overnight sensations and trouble makers and Sheikh Rabee[may Allah preserve and protect him] said that is general criticism.

[10] https://www.youtube.com/watch?v=7ck6Nj4AQsI&list=PLrym_grlN1V9RyUrWX_ZL_C_979FgBiyY&index=3

[11] https://www.abuaaliyah.com/2015/08/22/cult-characteristics-among-the-salafis-in-the-west-2/

The Conscience Awakening: Real Testimonials of those who left the Neo Salafy Cult Movement.

I also read the article about the cult like traits about a week ago, and brother every single word of it strikes home. Hard. I have been trying to get other people to look at it. But you are a "hizbi", "they" claim, so people won't read it unless they are already aware of the whole situation. In shaa Allah, some people that are still blind followers will read it and wake up.

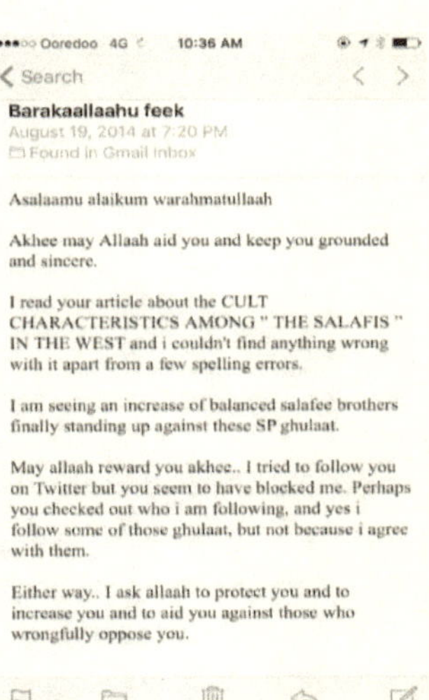

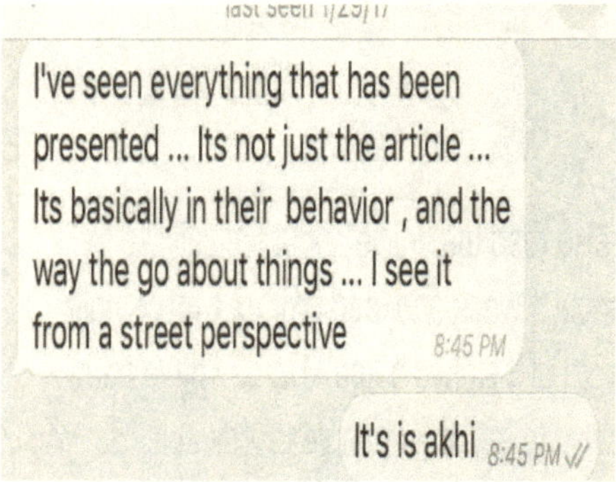

last seen 1/29/17
I've seen everything that has been presented ... Its not just the article ... Its basically in their behavior , and the way the go about things ... I see it from a street perspective
8:45 PM
It's is akhi
8:45 PM

last seen recently

January 11

Asalaamu 'alaikum brother, I just want to thank you for posting that info the last few days regarding Spubs. May Allah reward you .

I must admit I was angry and disgusted at the beginning but that was due to my ignorance as I have been out of the salaf community for a very long time and was unaware of all the politics etc. And have just come back into my dīn alhamdulillah -

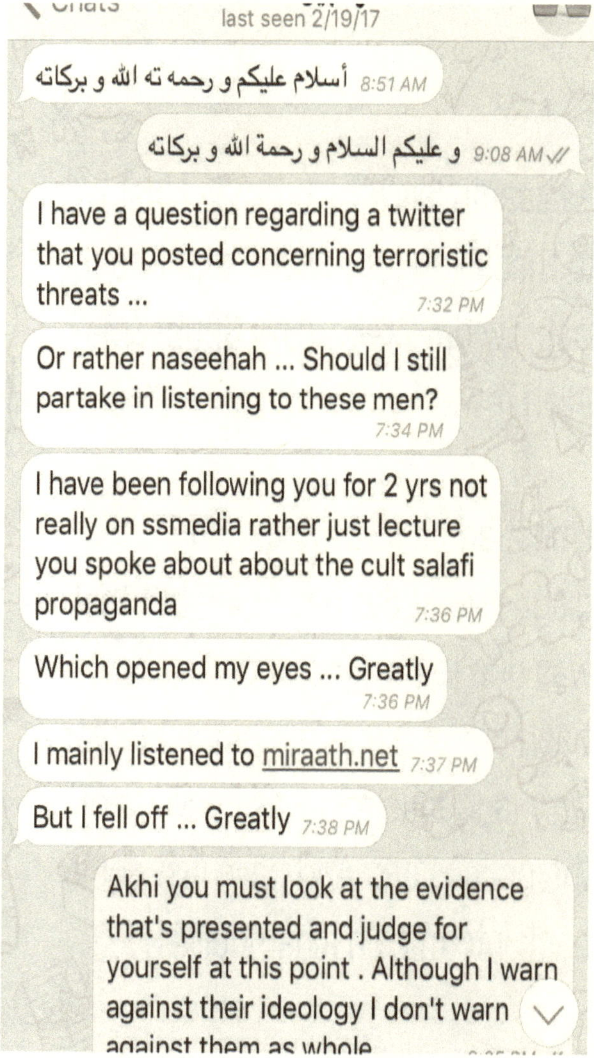

أسلام عليكم و رحمه ته الله و بركاته 8:51 AM

و عليكم السلام و رحمة الله و بركاته 9:08 AM ✓✓

I have a question regarding a twitter that you posted concerning terroristic threats ...
7:32 PM

Or rather naseehah ... Should I still partake in listening to these men?
7:34 PM

I have been following you for 2 yrs not really on ssmedia rather just lecture you spoke about about the cult salafi propaganda
7:36 PM

Which opened my eyes ... Greatly
7:36 PM

I mainly listened to miraath.net 7:37 PM

But I fell off ... Greatly 7:38 PM

Akhi you must look at the evidence that's presented and judge for yourself at this point . Although I warn against their ideology I don't warn against them as whole

One bro sent this to one of the bros
11:59 PM

The above is quite sad to see. The brother who wrote the article is salafi as far as I know. And the article is knowledge based yet abu khadeejah isnt responding to the issues raised in a knowledgeable way I suppose if he was a proper student of knowledge he would have. It comes across as just ranting and raving. Talking about someone's sins like that isn't how our scholars teach us to behave. Even if the brother did whay is begin claimed we shouldn't bring it up just in case he wasn't aware that it was public knowledge. We should deal with the issues not character assassinate anyone that tries to advise. If he's wrong lets prove him wrong based on knowledge not sensationalism. Allahulmustaan.

السلام عليكم أخي الكريم
أحبك في الله

I recently came across your pieces "cult characteristics among the salafis in the west"
& the commanality of Takfeer and Tabdee"
8:09 AM

JazakAllahu khairan
For dealing with this issue in a knowledge based way and not stooping down to the level of our dear bros
8:10 AM

Unfortunately they have had their way for far too long and dragged the name of the salaf as-salih and their way through
the mud harming and destroying individuals and the dawah.
8:12 AM

Chats
last seen 2 hours ago

September 30

Assalamualaykum 2:27 PM

Jazakallah khayr for the latest article
2:27 PM

May Allah reward you 2:27 PM

We facing a similar issue with a bro
here in Finland
2:28 PM

Who came with us from Nigeria 2:28 PM

Terrible akhee 2:28 PM

Chats
last seen yesterday at 9:52 PM

و جزاك الله خيرا 1:16 AM

Aki 1:48 AM

JzakhAllah khaire there are some.very
good benefits on your channel 1:49 AM

Ma sha Allah aki your case study on
hizbiyyah in the west was very
beneficial 1:51 AM

Abshir my brother you are not alone
many many in sha Allah balanced
salafis are against this hizbiyyah and
fanatacism and opression 1:52 AM

I ask.Allah to grant u ikhlas and
Blessings in.your affairs 1:55 AM

I.apreciate u must be busy but
from.time to.time.I.will try mesage you
ocasionaly maybe I have a question
whether is be realted to the science of
ahadeeth.Or perhaps an issue that
perhaps you have a benefit in or just
u.could help.me. 1:57 AM

We ask.Allah to.make.us.from those

Message

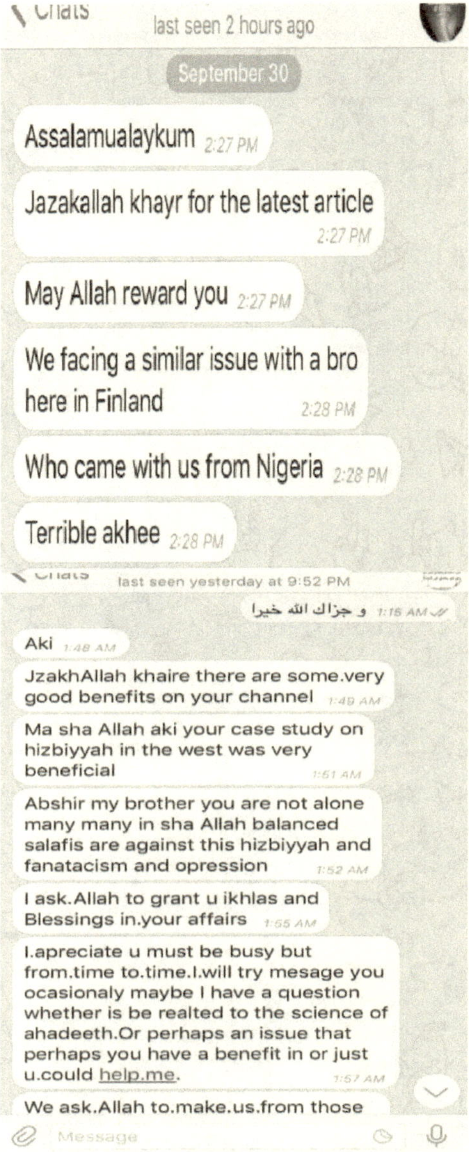

153

To: Dwight lamont Battle   Details

Wa Alaykum As Salaam,

JazakAllah Khair I am well, InshaAllah you are too.

I read with interest your papers and found them to be erudite and exactly how I have been feeling. My own experience leads me to feel that to become part of them it takes a shutting down of critical thinking and I have witnessed myself the damage they bring to communities under the guise of spreading the truth which then endeavors to silence discussion. I have personally lost friends over my refusal to accept YouTube clips and soundbites as refutation of individuals.

< Inbox (11)
               request for pdf   \ /

I have also seen those who were, lets say for the sake of ease "Jihadis" cross over into the neo-salafi group which leads to a toxic mix of ignorance and intolerance. I can't say this is across the board but it is definitely my experience. Even within their study groups the emphasis is on loyalty to the "Manhaj" I found that when I was within this group although very much on the periphery I felt that I had to conform and this was done with a subtlety that is quite amazing, the use of Islam as a controlling tool has led to many a burn-out and leaving to join Sufism.

It has become a brand within the UK which brings very polarising opinions amongst the general community even in my little town of Milton Keynes, although I do feel that they are losing legitimacy I just hope that the Dawah can recover quickly with the grace of Allah and the work you are doing I feel goes some way to re-balancing the fact that the Manhaj As Salaf stands for Justice and the correct Middle way.

May Allah Keep us steadfast upon his deen. Ameen

Ma Salaam.

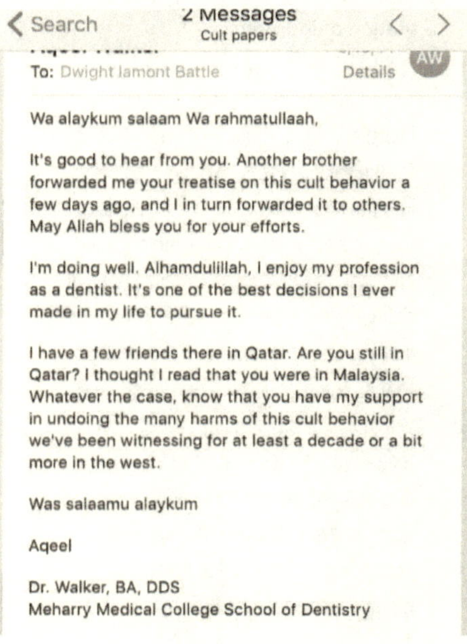